This book is a courageous, countercultural invitation to return to the joy that already lives inside you.

Tony Child, World-Leading Mindset Coach

AUDACIOUS JOY

The Keys to Living with Freedom, Authenticity and Unshakable Happiness

NICOLE KERNOHAN

TEDx Speaker and High-Performance Coach

Printed in the United States of America. Orders by U.S. trade bookstores and wholesalers. Manufactured and printed in the United States of America.

Orders by U.S. trade bookstores and wholesalers.

Manufactured and printed in the United States of America and distributed globally by Integrity Publishing International.

Publisher: Integrity Publishing International
Email: *Team@IntegrityPub.com*
www.IntegrityPublishingInternational.com

Paperback ISBN: 978-1-964330-32-7
Hardback ISBN: 978-1-964330-33-4

Testimonials

"Nicole Kernohan shows how the words we choose and the beliefs we hold shape the reality we live. Audacious Joy invites you to open your mind, rewrite your inner story, and experience life through the lens of joy."

— Dr. Joe Vitale, "Mr. Fire," Author of The Attractor Factor & Zero Limits

"I've worked with thousands of high achievers—from NFL athletes to CEOs—and I've never met someone who embodies joy more fully than Nicole Kernohan. Audacious Joy is a guide to study, live, and return to whenever you need to remember who you are."

— Tony Child, Entrepreneur, World-Leading Mindset Coach

"In Audacious Joy, Nicole Kernohan reframes joy as more than a fleeting emotion. Through powerful insights and practical tools, she reveals how changing your words, perspective, and habits can unlock a deeper, more sustainable, joyful way of living."

— Dr. Lorry Leigh Belhumeur, Ph.D., Psychologist & Author of Mastering Resilience

"Audacious Joy is a roadmap for rewiring how you see yourself. Nicole Kernohan gets to the root of transformation: identity. She connects mindset, language, and emotional truth in a way that's both grounded in science and rich in human experience. As someone who's helped thousands optimize body and mind, I can tell you... lasting results start here. This is the real work."

— Tara Garrison, Founder of HIGHER, Health & Life Coach

"In my years working alongside Bob Proctor, I've seen countless people talk about growth. Few embody it like Nicole Kernohan. Audacious Joy offers a refreshing, practical perspective that will challenge you to think differently and live more authentically."

— Bill Banta, Co-Founder, Elevated Alliance, CEO of Elevated Worldwide

"Audacious Joy is more than a book—it's a wake-up call. Nicole doesn't just write about joy, she embodies it. Her words remind us that joy isn't something to chase; it's who we already are."

— Maresa Friedman, Fortune 100 Strategist

"Nicole embodies these words from her book, 'Joy is the light we radiate.' In Audacious Joy, she challenges you to think and to do differently for true and lasting growth. If you are wary of the hustle and grind culture, read her word... heed her wisdom as she guides with an approachable vulnerability to help you live with deep joy as a state of being."

— **Susie Albert Miller, MA, MDiv, Leadership & Communication Strategist, & Author of Listen, Learn, Love**

"WOW! Grab this book today! Audacious Joy is a powerful guide that blends real stories with practical strategies for your success in life. Nicole Kernohan's message is authentic, uplifting, and contagious, the kind of book that makes you want to step up and live more fully."

— **Speaker Erik Swanson, 33 Time #1 Bestselling Author & Award Winning Speaker**

"As CrossFit owners, we see every day how physical strength and mindset go hand in hand. In Audacious Joy, Nicole captures that connection beautifully, showing how the words you use and how you see yourself influence not only your health but every part of your life. She brings the same warmth, authenticity, and encouragement to these pages that she brings to every class and conversation."

— **Dan & Ronda Stewart, Co-Owners, CrossFit Elgin**

"A fascinating inside look at what it takes to overcome major adversities, shift your mindset, experience exponential growth, and to show up in life with a light shining brightly. Audacious Joy is packed full of deep insights and actionable practices that you can incorporate into fueling your own personal and professional growth right away! This book is a must-read for anyone ready to step into a higher level of joy and success."

— Fred Moskowitz, Fund Manager, Bestselling Author, & Client of Elevated Worldwide

For Bob Proctor,
Whose words awakened something in me
a decade ago that I can never unlearn.
You reminded me who I am and what I'm capable of,
igniting a journey that continues to touch lives
far beyond my own.

Contents

WHY I WROTE THIS BOOK

For as long as I can remember, I've been fascinated by the quiet power of joy, the way it can transform a moment, a conversation, a life. Not the loud, flashy happiness the world often chases, but a deeper, bolder kind of joy that lives within us and moves through us.

Many people use the words joy and happiness interchangeably, yet they aren't quite the same. Happiness depends on circumstances, it's reactive and fleeting. Joy is quieter, deeper. It's not something you chase; it's something you allow.

Happiness often shows up when something good happens to you. Joy shows up when something good awakens within you. Joy lives inside you—it's that moment of peace that arrives even after tears, the whisper that says, I'm okay, even when circumstances aren't.

For a long time, I didn't even know how to articulate it. I just knew there was something real and important about that feeling, something I was meant to understand more fully. That quiet nudge led me on a journey of learning, growing, and discovering what it truly means to live audaciously joyful.

I wrote Audacious Joy because I believe we are all meant to live with that light fully turned on. I believe that joy is not reserved for perfect moments or perfect people—it's available to all of us, right now, no matter our circumstances.

This book is for the dreamers, the builders, the seekers, and those who know there's more waiting within them. It's for anyone who wants to stop dimming their light and start living with presence, authenticity, and bold joy.

My hope is that these pages remind you that you are powerful, you are a light, and you are capable of creating a life more beautiful than you've ever imagined.

Joy is not something you have to find. It's something you already are.

Thank you for trusting me to walk this journey with you.

— **Nicole**

TONY CHILD

Audacious Joy. These two words epitomize the life of my dear friend Nicole Kernohan. I first met Nicole while working alongside Bob Proctor, a man who spent his life teaching the world how to think differently and live differently. From the beginning, I could tell Nicole was different. Where most would show up at Bob's events to just gather information, she was there to transform. Her hunger to learn, to apply, and to live the principles being taught was evident. I could see it long before she could, that she was meant to teach this information to the world. Why? Because she was the embodiment of everything we were learning from Bob.

Nicole made the bold decision to leave behind everything she had been working on and step fully into this calling: to share with the world the power of mindset, emotional intelligence, and joy. I've worked with thousands of high achievers from NFL athletes to Olympians to CEOs and founders of companies, and I can honestly say I have never met someone who embodies the word joy more fully than Nicole.

Joy is one of those words that gets tossed around in our culture. We see it printed on mugs and stitched on pillows, but rarely do we see it lived. With Nicole, you FEEL it when you're around her. Years ago, I sat with her to write her personal purpose statement, a process I guide many leaders through. While in the process, I really focus on finding the word that radiates from someone's soul. Some examples of those words are freedom, love, adventure, and a myriad of other words. It usually takes me 15-20 minutes to grasp the word with someone. I only needed three minutes before the word came to me for Nicole. The word was simply *sunshine*. That's who she is. That's how she shows up. Sunshine. Nicole radiates light and warmth, and when you leave her presence, you carry some of it with you. It's contagious.

That's exactly what this book is about. It's about radiating Audacious Joy like sunshine. This joy isn't just happiness (which is the word the world will use sometimes to describe it). It's the kind of joy Nicole teaches as a bold, deliberate way of living. A joy that is not dependent on circumstances, but chosen in the face of them. She writes, "Joy doesn't happen to you; it happens through you. It's a choice, a state of being, and a way of living authentically in a society that often encourages us to dim our light." This is Nicole's life.

When I first read Nicole's story about being diagnosed with multiple sclerosis at the age of twenty-one and experiencing paralysis on the right side of her body, I felt it in my soul. I could immediately relate. My mom also had MS. In fact, two years before I was born, my mom woke up one morning completely paralyzed from the neck down. Back then, we didn't have as many research or treatment options for this debilitating disease as we do now. Over time, she regained feeling on her left side, but the entire right side of her body remained paralyzed for the rest of her life.

I grew up watching the daily battles she faced. MS shaped the way she lived, and it shaped the way I saw resilience, suffering, and strength. So when I read Nicole's words about laughing with friends in the hospital hallways, or choosing joy at the dinner table even when she couldn't lift a fork without spilling food, it was deeply personal for me. "How could someone laugh at something that brought so much pain and suffering to my mom?" I thought as I read Nicole's story in this book. I know what MS can take from a person. That's why Nicole's message of choosing joy in the face of adversity is so powerful. She has lived joy in the face of massive adversity.

That's why this book matters now more than ever. We are living in a world where anxiety, distraction, and comparison have become the norm. People are chasing external validation and wondering why happiness slips through their fingers. Nicole offers a different path. It's a courageous, countercultural invitation to return to the joy that already lives inside each of us. She shows that joy is not about ignoring pain or pretending life is perfect. It's about authenticity, presence, and remembering that your light has never been lost, even if the world has tried to dim it.

With over a decade of studying the mind, emotional intelligence, and personal transformation, she has both the expertise and the lived credibility. But more than her résumé, it's her character that makes these pages powerful. As already mentioned, she's not just another guru teaching others something she doesn't have. It's who she is at her core.

The following pages will transform you if you'll let them. Nicole gives you practical tools, like Progressive Affirmations, that help rewire your inner dialogue. She shows how to shift habits and language in ways that build an identity rooted in joy, rather than fear or lack. She reminds you that your smallest moments, like smiling at a stranger or listening deeply to a friend, can carry influence far beyond what you imagine. She demonstrates how choosing joy becomes an act of service. Her consistent choosing of joy in her own life has given her the credibility to write a book to help me and you do it as well.

My encouragement to you is simple: this isn't another book to be skimmed through and placed on a dusty bookshelf. It's a life manual to be studied in depth and absorbed. Let it challenge you. Let it reframe the way you see yourself and the way you see life because what Nicole is offering here is a blueprint for living.

By the time you turn the last page, I believe you'll see what I've seen in Nicole all along: joy isn't something you chase. Joy is who you are and living from that place with audacity, authenticity, and courage changes everything.

So lean in. Turn the page. And let Nicole remind you of the sunshine you already carry.

— Tony Child
Entrepreneur, World-Leading Mindset Coach, Teacher

CHAPTER 1
THE CONTAGIOUS INFLUENCE OF JOY

. . . .

HOW TO INSPIRE OTHERS
BY LIVING YOUR BEST LIFE

Imagine walking into a room filled with people, some chatting, others lost in thought, perhaps a few feeling the weight of their day. Then, without saying a word, someone enters with an undeniable presence, radiating joy. It's as if they carry an invisible light, one that touches everyone around them. Heads turn, conversations shift, and suddenly, the room feels lighter, more positive.

There's something powerful about joy. It's a light that radiates from within and touches everyone around you. In psychology, spirituality, and even neuroscience, joy is often described as an inner state that's deeper and more enduring than happiness. Joy doesn't happen to you; it happens through you. It's a choice, a state of being, and a way of living authentically in a society that often encourages us to dim our light.

When I talk about living "audaciously joyful," I don't mean pretending that everything is perfect or forcing yourself to be happy all the time. Life is filled with challenges, and you don't have to ignore them—it's how you show up in the face of them. Living audaciously joyful is about presence, connection, and the choice to see life as a gift, no matter what's happening around you.

JOY, PRESENCE, & AUTHENTICITY

Joy is the byproduct of aligning your desires and actions with your values and allowing yourself to be fully present in the moment. Joy isn't just an emotion. When you're truly present, you experience the fullness of life without distraction, without judgment, and without needing to control every outcome. Presence creates the space for joy to exist, even in the small, ordinary moments of life.

And interestingly, joy also invites others to be present. Have you ever noticed that when you're fully engaged with someone, when you're making eye contact, listening deeply, and being present, it creates a sense of connection that's hard to describe? Presence is contagious, and so is joy. When you bring your full self into any situation, you invite others to do the same.

THE SMALLEST MOMENTS MATTER

One morning, I was out walking my dog around our neighborhood. It was a regular day, nothing unusual, nothing staged. As we rounded the corner, we crossed paths with a neighbor who was out for a walk.

As we approached, I offered a warm smile and said a simple, "Good morning." That was it, no big conversation, no elaborate gesture. Just a smile and a few kind words. As we passed, he bent slightly to speak to my puppy, and then, almost to himself, he said, "You look kind, friendly and bubbly, just like your mom."

I smiled again as we kept walking, but his comment stayed with me. It reminded me that our presence, even in the smallest, briefest moments, has the power to impact others. Without realizing it, in a few seconds, I had made a first impression that radiated kindness, friendliness, and joy.

What if we all moved through the world with a little more intention, offering a smile, a kind word, or a moment of genuine warmth, even in the simplest moments?

Most of the time, we'll never know the impact we make. But once in a while, someone says something, and we're reminded: joy is contagious, even when it's unspoken.

To truly live in joy, you also need to know who you are. Authentic joy comes from within, and in order to embrace it, you have to let go of external pressures and tune into what you truly value. This requires some introspection and honest reflection. What do you care about? What excites you and brings you peace, not because you "should" want it, but because it truly resonates with you?

Society is filled with expectations, and it can be hard to know the difference between what we value and what we've been told to value. For some, joy might come from pursuing a high-powered career or owning a beautiful home. For others, it might come from traveling the world, spending time with loved ones, or cultivating a simple life. There's no single right path, only what feels authentic to you. The more you understand yourself and your values, the more aligned your actions will become, and that's when joy naturally flows.

I recognize that I had some early advantages when it comes to joy. I was fortunate to grow up in a positive, supportive environment, and I don't take that for granted. My childhood provided a foundation of optimism and resilience, something I know many people do not experience. My parents instilled confidence and love in my sisters and me, leading by example through hard work, smart choices, and an entrepreneurial spirit.

And here's the deeper truth: no matter where you start, joy is part of who you are. We are all born with a natural light. We are all born "sunshines," radiating joy and wonder. For some, the world may dim that light more quickly or more harshly, but the light is never lost—and it's never too late to reignite it.

FROM EXTERNAL TO INTERNAL VALIDATION

One of the most important shifts in my journey was learning to let go of external validation and embrace internal joy. I'll admit, for a long time, I worried about how others saw me. I worried that if I showed up as my full, joyful, bubbly self, I wouldn't be taken seriously. I feared that others might feel uncomfortable or think that I wasn't being professional. So, like many people, I dimmed my light in certain spaces to fit in.

But as I grew older and more self-aware, I realized that hiding my true self wasn't serving me or anyone else. Authenticity is one of the greatest gifts you can give to the world. When I truly embraced my natural optimism and chose to show up fully, I realized something amazing: it didn't push people away. In fact, it drew them in. My joy inspired others to be more open, more connected, and more willing to embrace their own light.

Joy doesn't only impact your own life, it creates a ripple effect, inspiring those around you to live more fully, too. When you're no longer relying on others' opinions to feel good about yourself, your joy becomes an act of service. You're no longer looking for validation; you're giving it away freely by showing up as your true self.

JOY IN HARD TIMES

I'm not suggesting that living joyfully means life will always be easy. There will be challenges, hardships, and moments where joy feels distant. And the beauty of joy is that it doesn't disappear when times get tough. It simply shifts.

CHOOSING JOY THROUGH ADVERSITY

Later in this book, I'll share more about my journey with multiple sclerosis (MS) and the ways it has shaped my life. For now, I want to share a simple truth that revealed itself to me early on: it's possible to choose joy, even in the midst of a deep challenge.

When I was twenty-one, I experienced a sudden neurological episode that left the entire right side of my body paralyzed—my arm, my leg, and even part of my face. I was in my last year of university, and overnight, my world changed. I couldn't walk, couldn't write, couldn't drive. Doctors told me I may or may not regain functionality.

On the surface, it would have made sense to fall into despair. But something inside me refused to accept defeat. I chose to believe that I would heal.

It wasn't easy, and it wasn't instant, but even in the middle of the unknown, I chose to search for joy. Even there, in the sterile, uncertain hospital hallways, I made the decision to keep reaching for it.

Friends would visit me, pushing my wheelchair around the corridors as we laughed and joked. Sometimes, the hospital PA system would call out, "Nicole Fennell (my maiden name), please return to your room—your speech therapist is waiting," and we'd laugh about it. Even in difficult circumstances, joy found a way to sneak in.

When I returned home and began relearning simple tasks like eating, my hand would shake and food would often miss my mouth entirely, sometimes even flying onto the floor. My family and I laughed around the dinner table as I tried, celebrating the small wins instead of mourning the setbacks.

Of course, I had moments of sadness and grief. I'm human. But I didn't stay there. I let myself feel those emotions, and I kept choosing gratitude, humor, and hope.

One day, a friend asked me, "I don't understand how you can be so happy going through what you're going through. How are you able to stay positive?" At the time, I didn't even know how to answer. It was simply how I saw the world. It wasn't forced. It was a choice, one that felt as natural as breathing. That question stayed with me. It planted a seed that would shape the next twenty-two years of my life, and the work I'm now honored to share with you.

In the pages ahead, I will show you what I have learned: that joy is not blind optimism or naive positivity. It is a bold, deliberate way of living. A way of seeing the world, of seeing yourself, that transforms not only how you feel, but who you are.

Joy is a choice available to all of us, even when circumstances seem impossible.

It doesn't erase the hardship, but it changes how we experience it. It changes how we live.

SHARING JOY THROUGH SERVICE

There's another powerful way to spread joy: through service. Service is one of the most direct ways to step outside of your own concerns and connect with something bigger. It allows you to offer your unique gifts to others in a way that uplifts both you and the people you serve.

One of the most remarkable ways to improve your own life is to help someone else through a similar challenge to your own. It not only makes you feel good, but it often brings clarity to your own situation. You see things from a fresh perspective, and in that process, you help yourself by helping others.

For instance, if you're feeling depressed, help someone else who is also feeling down find peace. Or if you're facing a challenge in your business and you choose to help another business owner navigate a similar issue, you'll find that the insights you share often reflect back to you. The peace and joy circle back.

Living joyfully and authentically allows you to become a ray of sunshine, a source of light and inspiration for others. It starts with recognizing and embracing the unique qualities that make you, you.

Joy isn't something that happens by accident. It's a reflection of the way you see the world, and that vision is shaped by the words you use, both in your internal dialogue and in how you speak to others. The language you choose reflects your beliefs about who you are and what's possible for you.

Joy expands when it's rooted in clarity: clarity of who you are, your true purpose, and a vision that inspires you and pulls you forward. That's where we'll go next.

CHAPTER 2

LIVING ON PURPOSE

HOW CLARITY IN ORDINARY MOMENTS LEADS TO EXTRAORDINARY IMPACT

If the word "purpose" feels a little overused these days, I get it. It's become a buzzword in personal growth circles, business seminars, and even social media hashtags. But there's a reason it's everywhere, because when understood in a grounded, real-world way, knowing your purpose can change your life. From your achievement of goals to how you show up in ordinary moments, purpose isn't about some far-off ideal. Living on purpose is a way of being. It's the alignment between your values, your desires, and your strengths.

When you're in alignment, even the smallest action can feel deeply fulfilling. You start to experience clarity instead of confusion. You feel grounded, not scattered. Purpose gives meaning to your mundane, motivation to your mornings, and depth to your relationships. And the good news is your purpose is already within you; it's just waiting to be uncovered, claimed, and lived.

For me, claiming my purpose didn't happen all at once. It unfolded in stages: through curiosity, through struggle, through unexpected wake-up calls, and through the people who crossed my path at just the right time. Looking back now, the signs were always there. The seed was planted long before I even knew what the word "purpose" meant.

A CHILDHOOD SPARK: MY LOVE FOR TEACHING

If I trace my purpose back to its earliest expression, I find myself about nine years old in the basement of my childhood home, arranging chairs and handing out worksheets to my younger sisters and neighborhood friends. I wasn't simply playing school, I was genuinely lit up by teaching. I loved explaining things in a way they could understand and watching their eyes light up when something finally clicked. I created lesson plans. I graded pretend tests. I probably took it all far more seriously than they wanted me to. For me, it was something profound and joyful.

As I grew, that passion kept showing up in different ways. In my teens, I began teaching piano lessons and karate classes. I found deep satisfaction in helping others grow and develop, especially when they didn't believe they could do something at first and then discovered that they could. I didn't yet have language for what that meant or where it would lead, but I now see it was a thread, something essential to who I am that would keep pulling me forward.

At the time, I didn't dream of becoming a school teacher. I wasn't drawn to the traditional classroom. But I loved teaching in its purest form: helping someone grow into a version of themselves they hadn't yet met (or had forgotten). That thread has never left me.

THE MS DIAGNOSIS: A WAKE-UP CALL

The first major turning point in my life came suddenly and uninvited. I was twenty-one years old and in my third year of university when I began to feel a strange tingling on the right side of my body. At first, it was subtle, just an odd sensation. But it progressed quickly. I started to lose functionality in my right hand. I couldn't hold a pencil or zip up my jacket. Soon, walking became difficult, too. My right leg dragged behind me. The right side of my face even started to go numb. Over the coming week, my right side became fully paralyzed.

It was multiple sclerosis. MS. A chronic, unpredictable disease that affects the central nervous system. I was young, busy, and ambitious, and suddenly, my body felt like it was turning against me. It was terrifying. But it also woke something up in me. I had a choice: to surrender to fear, or to choose a different story. I remember deciding, almost instinctively, that I would not let this diagnosis define me. I was willing to accept the diagnosis but not the prognosis. And that decision changed everything.

I became obsessed with learning about the body, the brain, nutrition, and healing. I didn't come from a health background, and I hadn't studied this in school, but I threw myself into it with urgency and curiosity. I wanted to understand how to support my body from the inside out.

What started as a personal mission to heal became a doorway into something bigger. For the first time, I saw that maybe my own healing wasn't just for me. Maybe it could be part of something greater. Perhaps what I was learning could also help others.

FROM CORPORATE SUCCESS
TO A DEEPER CALLING

As I continued to heal and relearn to walk and write, I returned to university, finished my business degree, and eventually found myself thriving in the corporate world. I worked for a large company in marketing and business strategy, advancing through the ranks over a ten-year period. On the outside, it looked like success: promotions, pay raises, praise. On the inside, though, something felt off.

I wasn't miserable. I actually really enjoyed my career and loved the company. I liked the fast pace and the structure, and I was grateful for the experience. But I knew I wasn't living my purpose, not fully. During those ten corporate years, my interest in wellness didn't fade—it deepened. I found myself constantly reading about nutrition and fitness and taking weekend courses on holistic health. That knowledge, and my passion for sharing it, became too loud to ignore. So, I took a leap: I left the corporate world and opened a health food store franchise.

That decision felt huge. I combined my business background with my growing knowledge of nutrition and wellness. I brought in other health professionals and practitioners to create a space where people could get real help.

In the beginning, things were flying! Business was soaring, and everything seemed to be falling into place. Gradually, over the first two years, I started to notice that something still felt incomplete.

Clients would walk in, eager for a supplement, a new meal plan, or a health solution. We'd give them the tools, the protocols, the exact guidance they asked for. And then... they wouldn't follow through. They had all the resources. But 80% of the time, they weren't implementing them.

At first, I was frustrated. Then I got curious. Why weren't they doing what they said they wanted to do?

That's when I started to see the deeper pattern: it wasn't the food or the supplement. It was their mindset. Their language. Their beliefs. They were saying things like "I've always had a slow metabolism," or "I could never change my diet," or "I can't afford it," or "It's not me, it's just that I have this diagnosis."

AUDACIOUS JOY

That's when it clicked. I wasn't just watching people struggle with their health. It usually wasn't laziness. It wasn't a lack of desire. It was something deeper: I was watching people be limited by their beliefs and their identity. That's when I realized: true transformation doesn't begin on the outside. It starts in the mind. And that was the second most significant turning point in my life.

THE REALIZATION OF A DEEPER PURPOSE

I was frustrated—struggling, really. I cared deeply about my clients and wanted to help them succeed, but I knew I was missing something. I could give them all the tools and education, but if their internal dialogue didn't change, their results wouldn't either.

Then came one of the most pivotal moments of my life. In 2015, I attended a three-day virtual seminar with Bob Proctor. I didn't know exactly what to expect, but what unfolded felt like a lightning bolt of clarity. Bob spoke about paradigms, those subconscious programs that run our lives, and suddenly everything clicked. It was like someone had turned on the lights in a dark room. I remember feeling fireworks of excitement while also wondering how on earth had I never learned this before!?

After the seminar, I booked a call with Bill Banta, who had worked closely alongside Bob Proctor for many years. That conversation was a pivotal moment in my life. I told him what I had seen in my clients and what I was beginning to understand about myself: that we are not limited by our circumstances, but by our beliefs. I had some big goals for my life, and I knew I was barely touching the surface of what I could learn.

I decided to leave the natural health business behind and transition full-time into the Personal and Professional Development industry for my career! As I dove in, I asked Bill if there was someone else in Bob's circle who was really living this work, someone I could learn from. That's when he introduced me to Tony Child.

Tony would become a friend, mentor, and, eventually, a business partner. From the very beginning, Tony embodied what it meant to live on purpose. He was teaching mindset, but more importantly, he was living it. His example inspired me to keep going, even when things were hard. He saw something in me I hadn't fully owned yet: that I was born to lead, to teach, and to help others wake up to their own potential.

This was a professional pivot, and it was a calling. The MS diagnosis had been the first major turning point in my life, an awakening. But this, this was the second. The moment I realized I wasn't just here to help people be healthier. I was here to help people remember who they truly are, to reprogram limiting beliefs, and to live fully, freely, and boldly.

With Tony's coaching and guidance, we crafted my personal purpose statement to guide me: "The sunshine that radiates from my heart is an influence for good to all those around to feel free and at peace. I live to wake up the world to a powerful, loving, and healthy life by modeling that example for others to follow. As I free myself, I'm able to free the world."

That statement is the intention that I live by. Whether I'm speaking on stage, working with clients, walking my dog, or simply smiling at a neighbor, my purpose lives in every moment.

Today, ten years later, I am grateful to now work directly alongside Bill Banta and Tony Child, fulfilling our purposes!

CLARIFYING & VISUALIZING YOUR PURPOSE & VISION

Once you've aligned your desires, values, and strengths with which help make up your purpose, the next step is to clarify your vision. A Vision is an inspiring goal that is aligned with your purpose. It reflects what you feel called to create, experience, and contribute.

And as Tony Child has defined it, purpose is your "why," and vision brings your "what" to life. It gives form to your goals and direction to your actions. When your vision is aligned with your purpose, every step you take, even the ordinary, seemingly small ones, becomes intentional and powerful.

A **vision board** can help with this clarity. It transforms an internal calling into an external focus, something you can see, engage with, and feel emotionally connected to. Some people dismiss vision boards as "fluffy" or superficial. But when created from a foundation of deep clarity and purpose, they become a powerful mechanism to focus your subconscious mind and daily actions.

Vision boards are not about cutting and pasting magazine clippings and hoping for the best. They're about aligning your energy, your beliefs, and your imagination with the life you're actively creating. It's not a wish list—it's a visual contract with yourself, a representation of the impact you're here to make and the version of you that will achieve it.

In his book, *The Magic of Thinking Big*, Dr. David Schwartz emphasizes the importance of visualizing your goals in vivid detail and attaching emotion to those visions. Similarly, the book *You²* by Price Pritchett introduces the idea of suspending disbelief, allowing yourself to entertain the possibility of something extraordinary, even if you don't yet fully believe in it. These principles are foundational in using vision boards with purpose and power.

GRATITUDE: THE STARTING POINT OF DESIRE

Before you try to map out your vision or uncover your purpose, it helps to begin from the right emotional state. And one of the most powerful places to start from is gratitude. As I've learned over the years, working with Tony Child and through coaching others, gratitude helps quiet the voice of lack and fear. When we try to create from a place of "I need this to feel whole" or "something's missing," we're not really visioning; we're reacting. True vision comes from inspiration, not desperation.

Napoleon Hill said it best in *Think and Grow Rich*: "Desire is the starting point of all achievement, not a hope, not a wish, but a keen pulsating desire which transcends everything." In my experience, that kind of desire is clearest when it grows from gratitude. Because when you start from appreciation, when you pause and look around at what's already good, even if it's small, you shift into a more open and creative state. And from there, your desires become clearer and more grounded.

You'll find a full chapter later on that dives into gratitude more deeply. For now, I want to encourage you to slow down before you define what's next. Let yourself see what's already working. Let yourself feel grateful. From that space, you can ask: "Now that I'm aware of all I already have… what more would I love to have? To experience? To do? To give?" That's when visioning expands instead of constricts. And that's when your purpose starts to speak more clearly, because you're quiet enough to hear it.

TAPPING INTO THE FEELING OF DESIRE

One of the most important elements of visioning is emotional intensity. You want to picture your dream and write it down, but also truly *feel* it. That feeling of anticipation, excitement, and connection can ignite something powerful. One of the clearest examples in my life came from when I first started dating my husband, Dave.

At the time, we worked in the same department of a large office. Our cubicles were right next to each other, and we both felt the spark, but also knew it might be complicated. We kept saying, "We shouldn't date... we work in the same department... this isn't the right time." But the more we tried to push it aside, the more the energy between us grew. It was almost magnetic. I'd find myself thinking about him constantly. When would I see him again? Would we talk that day? Every interaction felt charged with possibility.

Shortly after we quietly started dating, I moved to a different department, and it no longer felt like something we had to tiptoe around. But what stands out most from that time isn't only the relationship, it's the intensity of emotion I experienced. It was desire, connection, and curiosity—a kind of focus and excitement that took over my thoughts in the best way.

That's the kind of emotional connection you want to tap into when you're visioning your life. You don't need to be in a romantic relationship to access it. You need to allow yourself to *want* something deeply, and then let yourself *feel* like it's already happening—as if it's real now. That subtle shift, from wanting something in the future to embodying the gratitude of already living it, is what makes the vision magnetic.

This is about creating a space within yourself where you feel connected to what you're building. The more you practice experiencing your desires with that level of presence and belief, the more your vision begins to take form, because you're not chasing it from a place of lack. You're stepping into it from a place of truth.

A REAL-LIFE REMINDER: THE KITCHEN VISION THAT BECAME REALITY

At one point in my journey, I created a vision board with images representing different areas of my ideal life, including a specific image of a dream kitchen. It featured white cabinetry, an island with wood-toned accents, pendant lights hanging over the island, and a window over the sink that looked out into the backyard. I could clearly see myself standing at that sink, looking out the window, watching my son play with his friends. I felt it. I believed in it. I returned to that image over and over again, visualizing it as though I already lived in it.

Time passed, and we eventually sold our home. In the midst of staging the house for sale, I packed away the vision board. After selling, we moved in temporarily with my in-laws while we built a new home in the same city. With the chaos of moving, parenting, and designing a custom house during COVID, I forgot all about the specific images on that vision board. I wasn't consciously trying to recreate anything, I was simply choosing what I liked and making decisions based on what felt right at the time.

We had help from our home designer, Joanne, who guided us through all the lighting and interior selections. I remember walking into the lighting store and being drawn to a particular set of pendant lights for the kitchen. Without hesitation, Joanne said, "Those are exactly the ones I had in mind for you." With hundreds of options available, it felt serendipitous. We didn't even look at others. We just chose those.

This moment reminded me of a story I heard from John Assaraf in *The Secret*—the book and movie that introduced so many people to the power of vision boards. He shared that years after making a vision board with a picture of his dream house, he found himself moving into the exact house, only realizing it when he came across the old board while unpacking. I remember hearing that story and thinking, "That's wild." But here I was, experiencing something almost identical.

A few months after moving into our new home and unpacking, I came across my old vision board again and put it in my home office. A few days later, our new cleaning lady saw the board and pointed at the kitchen photo, saying, "Wow, this vision board kitchen looks exactly like your actual kitchen." I was stunned. I looked at the board, then back at my kitchen. She was right. It wasn't just similar, it was nearly identical. From the L-shaped counter to the wood accents on the island to the exact pendant lights I had chosen with Joanne, it matched in a way I couldn't have orchestrated consciously.

That moment reminded me of how powerful our subconscious mind really is. I had implanted a vision so clearly that, even when the board was out of sight, the image remained active in my mind. I had taken action exactly towards my vision without even realizing it, because I had already "seen" it. I had felt it. I had practiced believing it. And eventually, it became real.

Vision boards work because they help you instill a clear belief about what's possible. They become a filter through which your brain scans for opportunities, connections, and decisions that will move you towards your desired future.

If you don't set a destination in your GPS, you'll never arrive anywhere new. When your vision is specific, however, and emotionally anchored and consistent, your mind will begin guiding you toward it, one trusting decision at a time.

VISION BOARDS AS A TOOL

When used well, vision boards can become a filter for decisive action, not simply a collage of pretty pictures or wishful thinking. They're about reinforcing clarity. Here's what I've found makes them most effective:

- **Choose Images that Resonate Emotionally with Your Purpose and Vision**: The visuals serve as anchors for how you want to feel and the identity you aspire to embody.

- **Engage with it Regularly so it Stays Active in Your Subconscious:** You don't have to stare at it for hours. A few focused moments a day is enough to keep the vision alive.

- **Visualize the Feeling of Living Your Vision, Not Only the Outcome:** It's the emotion that fuels belief, and belief is what turns vision into action.

WHY VISION & VISUALIZATION ALIGN WITH PURPOSE-DRIVEN LIVING

Your vision is more than a goal—it's a reflection of your purpose in action. When you align your vision with your purpose, every image, every idea, becomes a beacon. It helps you focus, stay motivated, and make decisions that reflect the future you're creating.

And this is where purpose-driven living becomes truly alive. Because the vision you hold pulls you forward. It shapes your thoughts, your actions, and even your self-image. It becomes a mirror of possibility, showing you what's ahead and, more importantly, who you must become to fulfill it.

Success, in my experience, isn't measured by what you've achieved. It's measured by how in flow and connected you feel as you grow into it. As Earl Nightingale famously said, "Success is the progressive realization of a worthy ideal." When you move through your days with a purpose that lights you up, and you move in the direction of a meaningful vision with intention, you're already living successfully. You're already living on purpose.

FROM SUNSHINE TO SIGNIFICANCE

When Tony Child and I created my purpose statement, "The sunshine that radiates from my heart is an influence for good...," it was personal. Sunshine means something to me. Because light is contagious. Presence matters. And when you live in alignment with your purpose and vision, you shine without trying.

You won't always feel ready. You may not have every detail figured out. Purpose is about showing up with clarity, choosing intention over autopilot, and trusting that even a small step can move something big.

When your purpose is lived, it's felt. And when it's paired with a meaningful vision, it becomes even more powerful. Together, they ripple outward, sometimes in ways you may never witness. When you live with clarity and conviction, you quietly give others permission to do the same.

LIVING WITH PURPOSE & VISION:
YOUR NEXT STEPS

If you're still in the process of discovering or clarifying your purpose and vision, take heart, it's not a race. It's an unfolding. With each insight, each reflection, you move closer to the truth of who you are.

This chapter wasn't meant to tell you what your purpose or vision should be. It's an invitation to pay attention—what lights you up? What breaks your heart? What strengths come naturally? What dreams won't let go of you?

Your purpose and vision need to be yours—personal, authentic, and make you feel alive!

And here's what I've come to believe: when you clarify your purpose and create a meaningful vision to move toward, something begins to shift. You start seeing yourself differently. Acting differently. Believing differently. You begin becoming someone new; it's always been there, but may have been hidden for a while.

The next chapter explores this transformation, how the stories we tell ourselves shape not only our beliefs, but our identity itself. Let's go there next.

CHAPTER 3

THE STORIES BENEATH THE SURFACE

WHERE BELIEFS & IDENTITY BEGIN

If joy is the light we radiate, then the beliefs we carry, and the identity we've built around them, determine how brightly that light can shine. Beliefs shape our identity, and identity shapes the way we show up in the world. In this chapter, we'll explore how the stories we've internalized affect our self-image, and how changing the words we use can begin to change who we believe we are.

Words are powerful, and they don't exist in isolation. Every word you speak carries an undercurrent of beliefs, feelings, and emotions. As a coach, I've come to understand that it's not only the words people use that matter, it's the beliefs and feelings behind those words. Whether they realize it or not, their words reflect a deeper emotional perspective that shapes their reality.

For many people, their success or struggle begins with the language they use daily. They express their beliefs through their words and actions, and those beliefs either propel them toward their vision or hold them back. The key to unlocking the power of words lies in understanding the beliefs and feelings behind them.

THE FORMATION OF BELIEFS IN CHILDHOOD

Much of what we believe about ourselves and the world was formed in our early years, long before we developed the ability to consciously filter information. Many personal development teachers, from Bob Proctor to Dr. Maxwell Malts, describe how our subconscious mind is wide open in our earliest years, absorbing everything without question. Between birth and roughly the age of seven, our subconscious mind is like a sponge. We're especially impressionable during this time because we haven't yet developed the ability to discern what's fully true or not. That's part of what makes these early years so powerful in shaping what we come to believe.

At this stage, the words we hear and the emotions we experience shape the core beliefs that guide us into adulthood. Whether we realize it or not, many of the limiting beliefs we hold today were passed down from those around us in childhood. Phrases like "money doesn't grow on trees" or "we can't afford that" might have been absorbed into your belief system at a young age, forming the foundation for how you view money, time, or success as an adult. These inherited beliefs often go unchallenged, yet they quietly influence our everyday decisions.

HOW WORDS CAN
SHAPE—& BREAK—YOUR SELF-IMAGE

While our beliefs often begin in childhood, there are moments when a single word or phrase, especially one said with emotion, can shift how we see ourselves.

I remember an experience in fourth grade that left a deep impression on me. At that point in my life, I wasn't aware that my ears stuck out more than others. My parents never mentioned it, and I had no reason to think of it as different or strange. Then, one day, a boy in my class, irritated by something I can't even remember, looked at me and sneered loudly, "Yeah, whatever, Elephant Ears."

It was the first time I'd ever been called a name like that. I felt an emotional sting, and it was as if, in that moment, my self-image cracked. Suddenly, I became hyper-aware that I looked different, and that difference was framed as something to be ashamed of.

From that day on, I stopped wearing my hair in a ponytail, making sure to keep it down to cover my ears. I was embarrassed and didn't even want to tell my parents what the boy said. My mom noticed the change; she knew that I suddenly didn't want to wear my hair up anymore, but she had no idea where that decision had come from or how deeply it had affected me.

That boy's words, delivered with irritation and spite, stayed with me. It might seem small. My adult self can look back and say, "That wasn't a big deal." But when we're doing identity work, we need to put ourselves back into those childhood moments. We need to remember what we made those experiences mean, and how they made us feel.

Sometimes we need to go back and let that younger version of ourselves know: *You're still amazing. You were always enough.*

It took me more than 25 years to fully understand the impact of that moment. I didn't realize it had affected my confidence or shaped my self-image until much later, when I began studying the subconscious mind, learning about paradigms, and working in this field. Only then did the dots start to connect, and I could begin seeing myself, and that moment, through a new lens.

The words that shape us aren't always negative, of course.

Fast forward a few years to Grade 8. I had an English teacher who gave us an assignment that involved presenting a concept to the class. I clearly remember what he said to me afterward.

He looked at me and said, "I think you have a good radio voice."

One sentence. And it stuck. Until then, I hadn't really thought about my voice at all. If anything, I thought maybe it was annoying, or at the very least, I'd internalized the message that I talked too much. I'd had teachers and others in my life say exactly that: "Stop talking." "You talk too much." So, I thought of my voice as a nuisance, not a strength.

But that teacher saw something different. He said it once, but it stayed with me for my lifetime. And when I later started university, there was an opportunity to volunteer at Radio Laurier, the university's student-run radio station. You had to speak about the school news and play music on the air. I wouldn't have even considered it… except that I remembered what that teacher said. He thought I had a good radio voice. So, I tried out, and I was selected.

That one sentence, "You have a good radio voice," helped me start to see my voice differently. It shifted my belief from "Maybe I talk too much" to "Maybe my voice is actually a gift." It gave me the confidence to use my voice more purposefully, first on campus, and eventually, on stages, in coaching sessions, and as I wrote this book.

BREAKING FREE FROM A NEGATIVE SELF-IMAGE

As adults, we often carry with us the beliefs formed during childhood. Maybe it wasn't a comment about your appearance, maybe it was about your behavior or your lack of certain skills. Something a parent, teacher, or friend said that made you feel less-than or inadequate. These moments may have felt small at the time, but they can leave deep marks.

The first step to breaking free from these beliefs is recognizing where they came from and that they don't have to define you. You can begin rewriting the internal narrative using new, empowering language. Even small shifts in how you speak about yourself can help rewire the emotional blueprint you've been living from.

THE ROLE OF LANGUAGE
IN REFLECTING BELIEFS

Words are tools for communication, and they are also mirrors of your inner world. When you say, "I'm terrible at this," you're not just expressing frustration, you're reinforcing a belief. And the subconscious mind doesn't argue. It simply accepts.

Here's why that matters: your mind operates on two levels. The **conscious mind** is the thinking mind, the part of you that uses logic and reasoning. It takes in information through your five senses: what you see, hear, touch, taste, and smell. But it's your **subconscious mind,** your emotional mind, that runs the show. It stores your beliefs, habits, memories, and self-image. Researchers and teachers often estimate that your subconscious mind controls about 93% to 97% of your thoughts, actions, and results.

Think of it like an iceberg. Your conscious mind is the small portion visible above the surface, what you're aware of. But the vast majority, the part beneath the surface, is your subconscious. It's deeper, more powerful, and quietly influencing almost everything you do, even when you don't realize it.

So, when you say something often enough with emotion, even casually, your subconscious begins to accept it as truth. That's why language is so important in shaping self-image. The phrases we use reflect the beliefs we hold, and those beliefs shape our identity.

The good news is this: words can also change beliefs. And as your beliefs shift, so does your self-image.

KARATE & THE POWER OF REPETITION

When I was nine, my parents enrolled me in karate. I didn't want to go—I wanted ballet or piano, but they insisted that my sisters and I learn self-defense.

At first, I was terrified. I was smaller than most of the kids, and I didn't think I was strong enough. I would timidly pull my punches, afraid of getting hurt or hurting someone else. And the internal chatter was constant: "I can't do this," "I'm too small," "I'm not strong."

But every time I said, "I can't," my sensei would gently, yet firmly say, "Yes, you can."

At first, I didn't believe him. Yet he kept saying it, with belief, with conviction, with emotion. Month after month, and eventually, I started to believe it, too.

That belief changed everything. I trained in karate for nearly ten years, earned my black belt, and became a provincial champion. I didn't have the physical size advantage, but because my belief shifted, so did my self-image and actions.

I no longer saw myself as the small, timid girl. I saw myself as capable, disciplined, and strong. That new self-image became the foundation for so many other things I believed I could do.

BREAKING GENERATIONAL BELIEFS

So how do we break the limiting beliefs we've inherited, not just from childhood, but from generations before us?

It starts with awareness. Pay attention to the phrases you say in passing, especially when you're under stress. Things like, "I'm never going to be able to afford that," or "I don't have time for this." These are more than statements; they're clues. They point to deeper beliefs that may not even be yours to carry.

You may have heard your parents say things like, "That's just how life is," or "You have to work hard for every penny." These beliefs might have helped them survive in their generation, but that doesn't mean they're true for you, or that you have to keep repeating them.

When you become aware of inherited language, you gain the power to question it. You can decide which beliefs you want to pass on and which ones stop with you.

THE POWER OF ASKING EMPOWERING QUESTIONS

One of the most effective ways to uncover and shift limiting beliefs is by asking better questions. Our minds are like search engines; whatever question we pose, the brain will try to answer. So, when we ask low-quality, disempowering questions, we get low-quality answers that reinforce old patterns.

Disempowering questions sound like:

• Why do I always mess this up?

• What's wrong with me?

• Why does this keep happening?

These kinds of questions trap your brain in a cycle of blame, shame, and discouragement. They pull your focus inward in an unhelpful way and activate your subconscious mind to find evidence that confirms your fears or flaws.

Empowering questions do the opposite. They gently redirect your mind toward growth, possibility, and self-leadership. They allow you to pause, reset, and shift into a more resourceful state, without denying reality.

Try asking:

• What's one small thing I can do today to move forward?

• What can I learn from this?

• How would the version of me I want to become handle this?

These types of questions invite your subconscious mind to look for solutions instead of problems. They give your brain a new assignment, one that opens doors instead of closing them. And over time, as you practice asking better questions, you build a habit of thinking in a way that supports your evolution. It's about directing your focus toward what's possible and reminding yourself that you have agency, even in hard moments.

THINKING IN PICTURES

The words we use create images in our minds. And those images shape the way we think, feel, and ultimately act.

Think of this: Imagine you're holding a glass of milk and walking across a balance beam. If your inner voice is saying, *"Don't spill it. Don't drop it. Don't mess up,"* what image flashes through your mind? Most likely, it's a picture of you spilling the milk or losing your balance. The very thing you're trying to avoid is what your mind is focusing on.

Now imagine a different internal script: *"Stay steady. You've got this. Walk with ease."* Instantly, the image shifts. You picture yourself calm, balanced, and in control.

This is how powerful language is. It builds the mental imagery that fuels your emotions and, in turn, your actions. Your subconscious doesn't filter out the *"don't."* It latches onto the dominant image, what you're focused on, and begins to associate it with your identity.

So, if your internal narrative is saturated with statements like "I'm not good enough," then the picture your mind paints each time you try something new is already tinted with doubt and defeat. But when your words begin to reflect a new possibility, even one you're only starting to believe, the mental picture begins to shift. And with that shift, you give yourself the chance to show up differently.

THE POWER OF "AND" INSTEAD OF "BUT"

There's a subtle shift in language that can create a major shift in how you see yourself, and it starts with replacing one tiny word: *but.*

We often use *but* to diminish progress, deflect compliments, or downplay effort. It sneaks into our language and quietly erodes self-worth. We might not even notice it, yet our subconscious mind does.

Consider this: **"You did a great job, but you still have a lot to learn."**

Now compare: **"You did a great job, and you're continuing to learn and grow."**

The first version feels like a backhanded compliment; it plants doubt right after the praise. The second version allows both things to be true: you did great *and* you're still improving.

Here's another one you might recognize in your own self-talk: **"Thanks, but I still have a long way to go."**

Instead, try: **"Thanks, and I'm continuing to make more progress."**

One dismisses the compliment. The other receives it and reinforces growth. It's not ignoring the desire to improve, it's honoring where you are while staying open to what's next.

Even in moments of self-reflection, the word *but* can chip away at your confidence: **"I'm doing my best, but it's not enough."**

Versus: **"I'm doing my best, and I'm learning how to navigate this."**

But implies you're falling short. *And* creates space for both effort and compassion.

These tiny word choices might seem inconsequential. Yet over time, they shape your inner dialogue—and your inner dialogue shapes your self-image. Shifting from *but* to *and* helps you speak to yourself like someone you believe in.

REWIRING BELIEFS: THE ROLE OF EMOTION

If you want a belief to truly take root, it's not enough to repeat the words, you have to *feel* them. Emotion is what gives repetition its power. It's the emotional charge behind your words that tells your subconscious mind, *This matters.*

You can repeat "I am confident" a hundred times, but if deep down you feel uncertain, your brain will tune out the words and believe the feeling instead. The subconscious doesn't respond to logic, it responds to emotion.

That's why even a small spark of belief, a moment of genuine hope or conviction, can start to shift your identity. When your words carry emotion, they leave an imprint. And that's where real change begins.

The more you practice speaking to yourself with compassion, intention, and even a glimmer of belief, the more your subconscious begins to soften its resistance. And little by little, a new story takes root.

The words you use with yourself every day are like bricks building your future. Some were placed there by others. Some you laid down without even realizing. And now, you get to choose what stays, and what gets replaced.

We'll explore this more in the next chapter with a tool I call *Progressive Affirmations,* a way to build belief step-by-step in a way your mind can accept. For now, remember this:

Your beliefs aren't permanent. Your self-image isn't fixed. The words you choose have the power to open new doors. And every time you change the story, even a little, you start to change your life.

CHAPTER 4
PROGRESSIVE AFFIRMATIONS

HOW SMALL SHIFTS IN WORDS CAN CREATE BIG CHANGES

By now, you've seen how language and self-image are tightly linked. The words you repeat, especially the ones you say about yourself, not only describe your reality; they begin to shape it. That's why a single phrase can change your entire perspective.

Imagine waking up in the morning and telling yourself, "I'm not a morning person. I'm so tired already." You're setting the tone for a sluggish, frustrating day before it even begins. What if, instead, you told yourself, "Up until now, mornings have been tough, and today I'm choosing to start with energy." That small shift in language opens up a new possibility; it doesn't magically erase all challenges, yet it does set you on a different path. That's the power of *Progressive Affirmations*.

Through years of personal experience, coaching, and study, I've developed an approach I call *Progressive Affirmations* to help people shift their perspective, one intentional word at a time. *Progressive Affirmations* meet you where you are today, and with each small adjustment in your language, they allow you to gradually shift your mindset toward more positive, growth-minded beliefs. These affirmations aren't about jumping from "I can't" to "I'm perfect". Instead, they're about creating a bridge, small steps toward greater belief in yourself and what's possible. I've used this approach with many individuals over the past five years, and the results have been profound.

UNDERSTANDING THE BRAIN'S REACTION TO WORDS

Our brains are wired to prioritize negative experiences, a phenomenon known as negativity bias. This bias, rooted in our evolutionary past, means that negative words or thoughts tend to leave a stronger imprint than positive ones. Neuroscientist Dr. Rick Hanson, author of *Hardwiring Happiness*, describes this beautifully when he says, "The brain is like Velcro for negative experiences and Teflon for positive ones."

The good news is that we can counteract this bias. Studies show that positive self-talk and affirmations, especially when repeated with emotion, can activate regions of the brain associated with emotional regulation and self-perception. Over time, this rewires our neural pathways toward more constructive patterns of thought and behavior.

Repeated exposure to negative self-talk, on the other hand, reinforces deep-rooted limiting beliefs. A child who is often told they're not good at math, for example, may carry that identity into adulthood, even if their actual skills improve. The belief lingers because it's been repeated with emotion.

Just as beliefs are formed, they can also be reshaped. Regularly practicing positive affirmations, especially ones that feel believable and emotionally resonant, can start to shift those internal narratives.

This is where *Progressive Affirmations* come in. They offer a gentle yet powerful bridge from the limiting beliefs we've internalized toward more empowering, supportive ones.

REWIRING YOUR BELIEFS THROUGH LANGUAGE

Every time you use intentional language, you send a signal to your subconscious about what to expect and believe. Over time, this repetition becomes reinforcement.

Let's say someone struggles with self-confidence in their career. Their internal narrative might sound like, "I'm not cut out for this. I'll never be successful." Introducing a Progressive Affirmation, something like, "Up until now, I've felt uncertain, and today I'm learning to believe in myself," creates space for growth without denying the current reality.

You're not pretending everything is perfect. You're speaking to the next version of yourself. With consistency and emotional connection, these new phrases begin to rewire your subconscious mind, making empowered beliefs more familiar, and eventually, more natural.

What begins as a small shift in language becomes a powerful shift in identity. And over time, the words you choose stop being something you have to remind yourself to say, because they've become how you genuinely see yourself.

EMBRACING NATURAL HEALTH: A PERSONAL JOURNEY

During my experience with MS, I found myself exploring avenues I had never considered before. Meeting with my medical team was crucial, and I also ventured into the world of naturopathic medicine, nutrition, and physiotherapy. It felt like stepping into a vast, uncharted territory. I began telling myself, "I'm open to learning," or "It's possible for me to understand this." These were affirmations of willingness. Looking back, these were my early forms of progressive affirmations, bridging where I was with where I wanted to be.

PROGRESSIVE AFFIRMATIONS AS A TOOL FOR CHANGE

Progressive Affirmations are a bridge between the limiting beliefs we've internalized and the empowering mindset we wish to develop. If you've spent years telling yourself, "I'm not good enough," it can feel inauthentic to immediately declare, "I'm amazing at everything." That's why Progressive

Affirmations work, as they acknowledge how you see your current reality while inviting in the possibility of growth.

A powerful Progressive Affirmation to start with is saying the words: "Up until now" and "I am choosing."

Instead of saying, "I'm not good at this," you might begin with, "Up until now, I've struggled with this, and today I am choosing to learn." That small change in language opens a door. It doesn't force a dramatic shift overnight, but it gently leads you toward new possibilities. Over time, these small affirmations build a foundation for a new, more empowering belief system.

A REAL LIFE-SHIFT: FROM CHAOS TO CHOICE

The way we speak about ourselves is powerful, especially when it comes to our identity. Often, the language we use to describe ourselves becomes so ingrained that we believe it to be fact. One powerful transformation I witnessed came from a client named Allie, who at the time introduced herself as "a shit storm attractor." That's what she believed about her life. She said it with a half-laugh, but underneath was real pain. She felt stuck in a cycle of chaos, one setback after another, and it seemed like the only consistent thing in her life was that something was always going wrong.

Her words reflected how she saw herself: someone things happened to. Someone who couldn't catch a break. And because that's how she identified, she unconsciously reinforced it. That language was forming her identity and her reality.

During our work together, I introduced her to the phrase, "Up until now…" followed by "I am choosing…" It didn't seem to feel awkward to her; she took the idea and ran with it! She used the new language actively, in conversations, in meetings, in moments when things felt hard. And little by little, her words changed. So did her confidence. And so did her life.

Today, Allie speaks differently about her circumstances and also about herself. She no longer calls herself a "shit storm attractor." She sees herself as strong, intentional, and worthy of a fulfilling life. And what's even more beautiful is that she still uses the language of Progressive Affirmations when new challenges arise. It's become a tool she carries with her, not because life is perfect, but because now she is creating it.

LETTING YOUR AFFIRMATIONS PROGRESS WITH YOU

One of the most powerful parts of this process is that your affirmations will evolve as you do. The goal isn't to repeat the same phrase forever, it's to build belief until you no longer need a bridge.

At first, you might say something like, "Up until now I've struggled with this, and today I'm choosing to see it differently." Once you begin to feel that shift taking root, you can drop the first part and say only the new belief: "Today I'm choosing to see it differently." And eventually, that may become: "This is how I see things now." It's a natural progression, and you don't need to force it. Just let your words change as your belief deepens.

Here are a few examples of how that evolution might unfold:

- **Mornings:** → "Up until now, I've had a hard time with mornings. And today, I'm choosing to start the day with more energy." → "I'm becoming someone who enjoys mornings." → "I love mornings."

- **Math or learning something new:** → "Up until now, I've struggled with numbers. And today I'm open to seeing it in a new way." → "I'm getting more confident with numbers." → "I'm good at understanding numbers."

- **Courage:** → "Up until now, it's been hard for me to speak up. And today, I'm choosing to practice courage." → "I'm becoming someone who speaks with strength." → "I share my voice confidently."

The shifts compound over time, even if they seem small at first. And as you keep choosing better words, you'll find yourself stepping into a stronger identity without even realizing when the change became permanent.

There's no perfect number of steps. What matters is that your language grows with you. Keep listening to your inner dialogue. Let it stretch and celebrate when you no longer need the softer version because you've stepped into something stronger.

SHIFTING FROM "I CAN'T" TO EMPOWERMENT

The words "I can't" are one of the biggest blockers to personal growth. Every time you say, "I can't," you're reinforcing a limiting belief. By catching yourself when you say, "I can't," and replacing it with a Progressive Affirmation, you shift from a place of powerlessness to one of possibility.

For example, if you catch yourself saying, "I can't get ahead in my business," shift it to: "Up until now, I've felt stuck, and today I'm choosing to explore new ways to move forward." This small change creates space for action and growth, rather than reinforcing stagnation.

VISUALIZATION: ADDING DEPTH TO YOUR AFFIRMATIONS

Visualization can add another layer of power to your Progressive Affirmations. When you speak these affirmations, try to imagine what the desired outcome looks and feels like. If you're saying, "Up until now, I've struggled with mornings, and today I'm choosing to feel more energized," take a moment to close your eyes and picture yourself waking up with energy. Imagine the light coming through your window, the freshness of the morning, and how you'll move through your day with ease. Maybe even add an image to your vision board!

Visualization helps create an emotional connection to the words, which strengthens the belief and accelerates the shift in mindset. Your brain can't always distinguish between what's vividly imagined and what's real, so when you practice visualizing a more empowered reality, it becomes easier for your mind to accept and believe it.

APPLYING PROGRESSIVE AFFIRMATIONS IN DIFFERENT AREAS OF LIFE

Health and Wellness: "Up until now, I've found it challenging to maintain a healthy routine, and today I'm choosing to take one positive step."

Career: "Up until now, I've doubted my abilities, and today I'm choosing to recognize my strengths."

Relationships: "Up until now, communication has been tough, and today I'm choosing to listen and express myself openly."

Self-Confidence: "Up until now, I've felt unsure of myself, and today I'm choosing to believe in my abilities."

Facing Fears: "Up until now, public speaking has made me nervous, and today I'm choosing to have courage and practice."

MINDFULNESS: CREATING SPACE
TO CATCH LIMITING BELIEFS

Mindfulness is a helpful tool in the process of applying Progressive Affirmations. It simply means slowing down enough to become aware of your thoughts and emotions without judgment. That might look like taking a walk in nature without technology, breathing deeply for a few moments, or sitting in a quiet bath and letting your mind settle. Mindfulness is presence. It's the practice of being still and present long enough to hear a higher thought, one that isn't just a habitual loop from your past, it's something clearer and wiser from within.

By practicing mindfulness, you create space to notice your limiting beliefs in real time. Instead of letting your automatic, negative self-talk run the show, mindfulness helps you pause, reflect, and choose a new path forward.

Mindfulness also helps you connect with your emotions. The next time you catch yourself saying, "I'm so overwhelmed," take a deep breath and ask, "What am I really feeling right now?" By naming the emotion and acknowledging it, you create a moment of pause, an opening where you can choose a new way forward.

ADDRESSING SKEPTICISM: WHY AFFIRMATIONS OFTEN DON'T WORK

One common critique of affirmations is that they don't work for everyone. And that's true, affirmations won't work if you don't believe them. If you're repeating, "I'm confident" while feeling deeply insecure, your brain will reject the affirmation because it doesn't align with your current belief system.

This is why Progressive Affirmations are a bridge. They don't ask you to make a leap from "I'm struggling" to "I'm perfect." Instead, they acknowledge where you are right now and gently lead you toward where you want to be. When you say, "Up until now, I've struggled with this," you're not denying your current reality. You're simply opening up the possibility for growth. This small, believable shift makes Progressive Affirmations more effective for people who find traditional affirmations too unrealistic.

Progressive Affirmations are a way to rewrite your inner dialogue with honesty, hope, and direction. They help you soften rigid beliefs, create emotional flexibility, and open the door to change.

In the next chapter, we'll explore what turns these shifts in belief into lasting change. Because while words can open the door, it's your habits that help you walk through it. The identity you're building needs structure to grow, and that structure is built one small, consistent action at a time. Let's dive into the power of habits and how they anchor the new story you're telling yourself.

CHAPTER 5

BUILDING STRONG HABITS

YOUR PATH TO CONSISTENCY & HAPPINESS

When it comes to creating long-term success in any area of life, whether it's health, fitness, career, or personal growth, habits are the secret to freedom. While many people think of habits as restrictive or mundane, they are the key to freeing up mental energy and focus. Once you've built a strong habit, it becomes automatic. You no longer have to waste time deciding whether or not to take action, it's simply something you do without thinking. It becomes part of who you are—your identity. This is why habits create so much freedom; they remove the burden of decision-making and allow you to focus on what truly matters.

Building strong habits is possible when you create systems and merge those habits with your identity. When you see yourself as the kind of person who exercises, makes healthy choices, or prioritizes focused work, your actions naturally follow. It is usually not about willpower or forcing yourself into rigid routines.

In this chapter, we'll explore the psychology of habit formation, how to leverage repetition and emotional impact, and the ways habits can set the foundation for consistency, productivity, and freedom. We'll also discuss the balance between following structured habits and staying open to intuition, knowing when to adjust and flow with life.

HABITS THAT STICK: THE POWER OF IDENTITY

One of the most important shifts in building long-lasting habits is how you see yourself. Your habits are deeply tied to your identity… the internal narrative and beliefs about who you are. Some refer to this as your self-image, especially when describing the outer roles or characteristics you associate with. But at its core, your identity is what drives your actions. If you want to build new habits, you must start by changing the story you believe about who you are.

In his book *Atomic Habits*, James Clear calls these "identity-based habits." Rather than focusing on what you want to achieve, he encourages you to focus on *who* you want to become. This subtle shift is powerful: when you believe you're a healthy person, you naturally make healthy choices. When you believe you're a disciplined person, consistency becomes easier. That identity shift is what makes the habits stick.

When I was diagnosed with MS, something inside me shifted almost immediately. I didn't know exactly what the path would look like, but I made a decision: I would heal, and I would look healthy doing it. I didn't identify as a victim. I saw myself as someone who was going to figure this out.

Looking back, I can see that even the decision to seek out naturopaths and nutritionists was a reflection of that new identity taking hold. I had always seen myself as someone who could create solutions and rise to challenges, so when this one came, I met it with the same internal belief.

The identity shift wasn't something I forced. It happened through the emotional intensity of the diagnosis and the decisions I made right after. In the next section of this chapter, I'll share two key ways in which identity shifts like this happen, through emotional impact moments *and* through repetitive emotionalization over time. These shifts are essential if you want to build habits that stick!

If you want to build new habits, begin by asking yourself, "Who is the person I want to become?" Then start acting and feeling as if you are already that person. Over time, your actions will reflect your new identity, and the habits will follow. You can also use progressive affirmations to build your belief in that identity.

PURPOSE: FUELING IDENTITY & HABIT CHANGE

Before diving into how identity and habit shifts are created through repetition or emotional impact, it's important to pause and connect with your *why*. Purpose acts like rocket fuel for both identity shifts and lasting habits.

When your intention is vague, like "I should work out more," it rarely sticks. And if it comes from a feeling of "I should" rather than "I want to" or "I choose to," it's rooted in lack or obligation. That energy doesn't lead to inspired, consistent action.

But when your habit is anchored in something meaningful to *you*, everything shifts. You're no longer trying to *do* something new. You're showing up for who you're choosing to *be*.

You're building strength so you can lift your kids or hike that trail you've dreamed about. You're setting boundaries because your peace matters. You're waking up early, both to be productive and to create space for the version of you that's ready to rise.

When your habits are fueled by purpose, they're not only easier to follow through on, they're more aligned, more joyful, and more sustainable.

So, before you focus on *what* you're doing, take a moment to ask: Why does this matter to me? Who am I becoming because of it?

SHIFTING IDENTITY THROUGH REPETITION & EMOTIONAL IMPACT

While the rest of this chapter explores practical strategies for habit formation, it's important to zoom in on two powerful forces that shape not only our habits, but our identity: **repetition** and **emotional impact**. Bob Proctor, one of my own teachers for seven years and a leading voice in the personal growth industry, often taught these are two of the most impactful mechanisms we have for shifting the way we see ourselves and, by extension, the way we behave.

As we explored in Chapter 3, your beliefs, especially those formed in childhood, become part of your **paradigm**: the deeply held subconscious programming that shapes your self-image, decisions, and behaviors. As Bob Proctor taught, your identity is part of that paradigm. And **shifting that internal pattern is what makes lasting change possible**.

The neat thing is, identity and habits influence each other in both directions. You can start from the inside by reshaping your identity through intentional language, emotional repetition, and visualization. As that internal self-image shifts, your actions begin to follow.

And you can also start from the outside in. Sometimes, it's your consistent actions, repeated again and again, that begin to **reshape** your identity. You might not feel like a consistent person at first. But every time you show up, every time you keep a promise to yourself, every time you follow through, you're proving to yourself: *this is who I am now.*

This is where repetition, especially when paired with emotion, becomes a bridge. It takes what you're doing and transforms it into who you believe yourself to be.

MY KARATE JOURNEY & THE POWER OF REPETITION WITH EMOTION

One of the most powerful examples of a meaningful shift in my identity and habits came through my experience in karate. When I first started karate as a child, I didn't immediately see myself as someone who could excel at it. I wasn't naturally strong or confident in my abilities. But something began to change the more I trained, and my sensei played a huge role in that transformation.

Every time I faced a challenge or doubted myself, my sensei would look at me and say, "Yes, you can!" He believed in me, even when I didn't believe in myself. That belief, repeated over and over with emotion, began to shift my own sense of identity. I started to see myself as a stronger girl, someone who was capable of doing karate well. The repetition of going to karate consistently, paired with my sensei's belief, helped me build habits of fitness, discipline, focus, and pushing my body beyond my perceived limits.

As I went to class regularly, it was more than learning martial arts techniques, I was building the habit of showing up and pushing through. Karate taught me to be disciplined in the dojo, and that rippled to other areas of my life. It was through the repetition of movement and the emotion of my sensei's encouragement that I started to see myself as someone who could be strong, focused, and determined. My identity shifted, and with it, my actions naturally shifted with that new self-image.

This experience is a perfect example of how identity shifts and new habits are formed through the combination of repetition and emotion. What made me strong was the combination of the physical consistent practice of karate along with the emotional reinforcement of my sensei's belief in me. Over time, I didn't have to think about whether I was going to show up for karate, I simply did it because it had become a part of who I was.

MS & THE LIGNTNING BOLT OF EMOTIONAL IMPACT

Some identity shifts don't happen gradually. They hit like a lightning bolt.

When I was diagnosed with MS, everything changed overnight. The moment was so emotionally intense that I almost instantly altered many of my habits, especially around food and health. I didn't wait to ease into it. I booked appointments with a naturopath. I began researching relentlessly. I wasn't born with superhuman discipline, but because the emotional impact was so profound, I **no longer saw myself the same way**.

I became someone who valued her health above all else. That new identity led to new habits. It was a survival-level shift, but one that opened up a whole new chapter of healing, ownership, and strength.

Emotional impact moments like this often mark turning points in life. But they don't guarantee positive change. Sometimes, they send people spiraling into fear or avoidance. That's why **awareness** is so powerful. When you experience a major life event, positive or negative, you get to decide what habits you create in response. Will they align with who you want to become? Or will they reinforce fear, limitation, or survival-mode thinking?

In the next section, we'll explore tangible strategies that can help you build habits with intention... no emotional lightning bolt required.

TANGIBLE STRATEGIES FOR BUILDING HABITS

Now that we understand the importance of identity-based habits, let's dive into practical strategies for building powerful habits.

1. Start Small (Two-Minute Rule)

A concept from James Clear's *Atomic Habits* is the **Two-Minute Rule**: any new habit should be so easy that it takes less than two minutes to start. For example, if you want to build the habit of exercising, start with two minutes of activity. The idea is to make the task so simple that you can't say no. Once you begin, it's easier to build momentum and continue.

I still use the two-minute rule with new habits today! Even with things that are already somewhat of a habit. For example, if I want to study a new concept but don't "feel like it," I will ask myself just to commit to reading for two minutes. I say, "When I study for two minutes, I can then go do whatever other things I wanted to do." It is surprising how many times I only require two minutes of myself but end up doing twenty minutes.

2. Make It Obvious, Easy, and Attractive

To build strong habits, you need to make them easy to initiate, obvious in your environment, and attractive enough to follow through. Here's how these principles work together in my example of starting to workout more consistently at the gym:

- **Make it obvious**: I laid out my workout clothes the night before, so they were the first thing I saw in the morning. This served as a visual cue to start my day with exercise.

- **Make it easy**: I followed a pre-determined workout routine and a specific timeframe, so I didn't have to think about what I was going to do once I got to the gym. This removed any mental friction.

- **Make it attractive**: I looked forward to seeing my friends at the gym, which added a social element and made the habit more enjoyable.

- **Make it rewarding**: After the workout, I felt a sense of accomplishment and had the benefit of social connection with my gym friends. The reward of feeling good post-workout made it easier to stick with the habit.

These small, intentional strategies are what make habits easier to form. When you set yourself up for success in advance, you reduce the mental and emotional friction that typically derails us from forming good habits.

A REAL HABIT LOOP IN ACTION

There was a time, years ago, when my son was around three years old, that I had built such a strong habit loop around going to the gym that it became almost automatic. On daycare mornings, my routine was always the same: I'd get up, put on my workout clothes, make my protein smoothie, feed my son, drop him off, and then, without even consciously thinking about it, I'd drive to the gym.

On more than one occasion, I found myself sitting in the gym parking lot before I even realized I was there. That's how automatic the behavior had become.

I remember one of those mornings clearly. I parked the car in the gym parking lot, turned off the ignition, and then thought, "Wait… I'm feeling tired and don't even want to exercise". I had moved on autopilot to the gym before "deciding consciously" if I was up for it. I paused and checked in with myself. I was a bit tired, but not overly so. I decided to go in and move gently, just do something. Not only did I end up getting a decent workout in, but I also left feeling re-energized and proud of myself.

To me, this was a powerful reflection of the habit loop working exactly as it should. I had created a system that made it obvious, easy, and even enjoyable to follow through. The gym had become part of who I was. I didn't have to force myself each time; I designed my environment and routine in a way that supported the habit with very little friction.

ACCOUNTABILITY: THE SECRET INGREDIENT

One of the most effective ways to build and maintain habits is to have an accountability partner. When you know someone is checking in on your progress, it's much easier to stay consistent. Accountability creates a sense of responsibility, not just to yourself, but to someone else. It adds an extra layer of motivation, especially on days when you're tempted to skip a habit or give in to distraction.

And here's the key: choose someone who will cheer you on *and* call you forward. You don't want someone who will let you off the hook or reinforce your old identity. You need someone who believes in your ability to shift, *even if you've tried and failed before.*

This doesn't have to be someone in your household; in fact, it's often better if it isn't. Whether it's a friend, mentor, coach, or colleague, the right accountability partner can reflect your potential, help you stay true to your new identity, and keep you moving forward, personally and professionally.

INSIDE OUT OR OUTSIDE IN:
BOTH LEAD TO LASTING HABITS

When it comes to changing your habits and creating lasting transformation, there's no single right starting point. Sometimes, the shift begins from within. You experience an emotional impact moment, or you intentionally repeat affirming words with emotion, statements like "I am strong" or "I am becoming someone who follows through", and over time, you begin to believe them. That identity shift paves the way for new habits to stick with more ease and flow.

Other times, it works in the other direction. You might start with small, consistent actions, even if you don't fully believe in the identity yet. You might follow a new habit loop, set up your environment for success, or use tools like the Two-Minute Rule. At first, it may feel like you're going through the motions. But with repetition, those actions begin to prove something to yourself. You begin to trust, *This is who I am now.*

Both approaches are powerful. And both are valid.

Repetition with emotion is one of the most potent tools for shifting identity, especially when it comes to the language you use. The words you hear repeatedly (from others or your own self-talk) carry emotional weight. Over time, those words shape how you see yourself. That's why affirmations, encouragement, and intentional language matter so much, they help you build the inner foundation that makes new habits easier to live out.

So don't wait for a lightning bolt moment. And don't assume your new identity has to be fully formed before you take action. You can start where you are. From the inside out or the outside in. The key is to bring awareness to what you're doing and an emotional connection to why it matters.

INTUITION & HABITS:
TRUSTING YOUR INNER GUIDANCE

As powerful as habits are for creating consistency and freedom, there's an equally important force to honour: your intuition. When you've trained yourself to follow through automatically, it's easy to assume you must stick to your plan at all costs. But sometimes, the most aligned action is the one that invites you to pause and check in.

A few days ago, and a few years after the ending up habitually in the gym parking lot scenario, I had planned to attend a 7 AM CrossFit class. I knew I was going to bed later than usual. Still, I had set my alarm, nothing blaring or jarring, just a gentle sound to wake me, and I went to bed knowing I'd decide in the morning whether to go, based on how I felt.

When I woke up, I noticed I was more tired than usual. My body was giving me subtle cues, and instead of overriding them out of habit, I paused. I asked myself: *What do I need this morning?* I didn't rush the answer. I tuned in and listened. And in that stillness, I knew, I could go. I would go. I didn't need to go all-out. I could take it slow, modify movements, and focus on moving my body with presence instead of intensity.

That small moment of choice felt deeply self-honoring. And by the time I left the gym, I felt energized, grounded, and grateful because I trusted myself.

This is the balance we're aiming for. Intuition doesn't mean abandoning habits on a whim. And commitment doesn't mean pushing yourself past what's true for you. The real growth is learning to discern the difference between excuses and intuition, between a needed rest and a fear-based retreat, between resistance that holds you back and alignment that calls you forward.

There will be seasons when honoring your body or your family takes priority. You may choose to rest instead of push. You may choose presence over productivity. And there will be times when following through, even gently, reminds you of your strength and steadiness. Both choices can be powerful. What matters most is that you're the one choosing.

The more you practice listening, the better you get at knowing. Trust your inner guidance.

FINAL THOUGHTS: CONSISTENCY, FREEDOM, & JOY

Building strong habits is the foundation of creating consistency, freedom, and joy in your life. When your habits are aligned with your values and goals, they free you from decision fatigue and help you stay focused on what truly matters. It's about consistency, intention, and creating those habits that reflect who you want to become. You have to be intentional, not perfect.

When your habits are rooted in intention, you create consistency and the capacity for ease, flow, and purposeful momentum!

CHAPTER 6

FROM HUSTLE TO FLOW

. . . .

UNLOCKING PURPOSEFUL MOMENTUM
WITHOUT BURNOUT

Imagine a society where success doesn't require burnout. For years, we've been conditioned to believe that results only come from pushing harder, working longer, and grinding through exhaustion. But what if that's not true? What if success is actually sustainable, when it comes from being in flow?

When I talk about "flow," I don't mean lounging by a lake with no responsibilities (though that can be part of it, too). I'm talking about shifting from hustle, where your energy comes from urgency, fear, or pressure, into a state of inspired action, where clarity and alignment guide your steps. Flow doesn't mean doing nothing. It means doing the right things from the right energy. When I say "energy" I'm referring to your attitude, beliefs or feelings. You're still taking action, but it feels different; it feels energized, grounded, and natural.

Moving from hustle to flow means shifting from force to alignment. You're still moving forward, but your actions aren't frantic or fear-based. Flow doesn't necessarily mean you're working less, sometimes it may, but it means you're working with intention and energy that feels natural and powerful. You move with presence, rhythm, and meaning. You still have big goals. You still have drive. But now, you're guided by alignment, not pressure.

For someone like me, an action-taker with an A-type personality, this has been a game-changer. I used to believe flow meant slowing down or doing less. But I've learned that being in flow can include momentum, deadlines, and productivity... without the anxious weight. Flow is about how you feel while you move forward. It's the feeling behind the doing, not the speed of the doing.

I used to joke: "I'd love to go with the flow... if someone could just tell me, what time does the flow start?" That line always made people laugh because they could relate. And what I've learned is that flow doesn't happen on someone else's timeline. It happens when we shift internally, when we're grounded, intentional, and clear on why we're doing what we're doing.

You can still have a color-coded calendar and a goal-tracking app, if you want them. The key is how you feel while using them. Do you feel grounded and energized? Or are you running on fear and pressure? There is a way to be productive and peaceful at the same time. It takes awareness and intention.

WHAT IS FLOW?

Flow is that state when everything clicks into place. You're still taking action, it simply feels more effortless, like you're being pulled forward by inspiration rather than pushed by deadlines and demands. Flow is about finding that sweet spot where your work is aligned with your purpose, and every action feels meaningful. It's a space where you're productive, but not at the cost of your well-being. Flow allows you to achieve more with less stress, and it leads to more sustainable success.

For many business owners, salespeople, and entrepreneurs, the idea of flow might seem abstract. They're used to pushing through, meeting quotas, and constantly moving to the next task. And flow doesn't mean you slow down to a crawl. You just find a way to move forward in alignment with your purpose and emotions, so your actions feel inspired, not forced.

For example, as I write this book, I'm in a state of flow. I'm not forcing the words onto the page, rather I'm allowing the ideas to come when they're ready. I write when I feel inspired, and the process feels natural, not rushed or pressured. There have been times over the past year, however, that I did feel some resistance or force around finishing this book. And I chose to follow my own guidance, to pause, be kind to myself, remember why I'm doing it, and pick it up when I either felt inspired or not in resistance and therefore open to getting into flow.

FLOW & THE POWER OF PURPOSEFUL ACTION

When a clear purpose guides your work, and your actions are rooted in trust rather than tension, everything changes. Tasks feel lighter. Decisions come more easily. Momentum builds naturally instead of needing to be forced.

About eleven years ago, I owned a health food store and was beginning to feel the nudge that my path was shifting. I had already started to consider leaving the business, but didn't quite know what was next. Around that same time, I attended a three-day seminar with Bob Proctor, and it was a wake-up call! I immersed myself in his teachings and decided that moving full-time into becoming certified, coaching, and training in personal and professional development was going to be my path. While still at the health store, I began learning and implementing tools that helped me view my business from a different perspective.

Instead of pushing to hit targets or trying to keep the business afloat by effort alone, I began applying what I was learning. I brought my team, each of them health professionals, into the process with me. Together, we created what we called a goal statement: a present-tense declaration of how we were serving, who we were becoming, and how it felt to thrive. We read it every morning, wrote it out by hand, and paired it with daily gratitude. These small but powerful actions anchored us in a new kind of energy.

We weren't frantically reacting to problems or chasing numbers. We were showing up with trust, clarity, and confidence in the impact we were making. I noticed how our interactions with clients shifted; we were more present, more engaged, and the clients responded. They got better results, and our business outcomes began to improve. It was like the entire environment changed when we stepped into flow, one rooted in service and belief instead of fear or scarcity.

Although it was powerful momentum, this shift came shortly before I officially transitioned out of the health food store business. I had already made the decision to follow my deeper calling and move fully into coaching and mindset work. But what happened during those last few weeks was undeniable. We saw real momentum building. The shift in our mindset created a shift in results.

And that experience stayed with me.

Flow, paired with purposeful action, both feels better and *works better*. When you take steps from a place of trust and alignment, you create more ease and more impact. You're still doing the work, but the energy behind it is different.

That's where true power lives.

THE TEDX TALK I ALMOST SAID NO TO

For years, the idea of doing a TEDx talk lived quietly in the background of my mind. It wasn't a set goal, just one of those "maybe someday" dreams. But every time it came up, it felt out of reach. TEDx talks were for bestselling authors, researchers, and viral speakers... not for someone like me. I didn't even know where to begin.

Still, the idea lingered.

Then in January 2024, I was invited by our business strategist, Maresa Friedman, to attend a high-level event called Secret Knock in California. I didn't have all the details, but I felt pulled to go, and I trusted Maresa. I said yes.

At that event, I met Erik Swanson, founder of Habitude Warrior, and John Kovach Jr., who works closely with him. They run a publishing and speaker development organization, and both would later play a key role in my journey. At the time, we had no formal plans, just a connection and a conversation about writing and speaking. Looking back, I realize it was one of those "coincidences" that wasn't a coincidence at all.

The week after the event, I had a conversation with Jon and decided to jump in and work with them on a co-authored book series and some speaking opportunities. Erik invited me to speak at one of their following events in Scottsdale, Arizona. Again, I said yes, still trusting the nudge, not knowing exactly where it would lead, but knowing it was in alignment with my vision and purpose.

While I was at the Scottsdale event, something powerful happened. I met two other speakers who had each already done a TEDx talk. I hadn't known they would be there. We connected in casual conversation, but what they offered me was more than tips on how to apply, they offered belief. They didn't question whether I could do a TEDx talk; they said, "Of course you can. You absolutely should." That kind of confidence from people who had already walked the path helped me move forward more quickly, with more flow and less hesitation. They gave me belief before I fully had it myself.

When I left the stage in Scottsdale, I felt something shift. I hadn't gone in thinking it would be a defining moment, but it became one. The energy in the room, the powerful feedback about my talk, the deep alignment with my message—all pointed to something greater unfolding.

I went home and got to work. I reached out to my strategist, Maresa, who had also done a TEDx, and I also enrolled in a short online course about how to apply for and deliver a TEDx talk. I researched locations, dates, and application timelines. I even started creating a spreadsheet to track which events I'd apply to and when.

Then, right before I submitted any applications, I got a call from Erik.

He had a connection to the organizers of TEDx St. George in Utah. Two speaker spots had recently become available, and he offered to recommend me and help submit my application...

as long as I was willing to go through the formal interview process.

Here's the part I'm not proud of: I almost said no.

Even though this had been a dream, my initial reaction was fear. The event was too fast. TEDx talks require a memorized script, intense preparation, and a polished delivery. I thought I needed a year to get ready. And even though I had already envisioned this moment, my inner dialogue sounded like this:

"It's too soon. I'm not ready. This location and timing weren't part of my plan."

I nearly self-sabotaged.

Self-sabotage occurs when you unconsciously block your own success, often due to fear of being seen, change, or receiving something you deeply desire. It's not because you're unmotivated. It's usually because you're scared of what the next level might ask of you.

That was me.

I teach people how to move past fear, and yet here I was, afraid to say yes to something I had literally visualized. In fact, I had even added a photo of a woman standing on a TEDx stage to my vision board just weeks earlier. She looked a lot like me.

After sleeping on it, I got clear. This opportunity wasn't random. It had arrived because I had already been in pursuit, saying yes, showing up, doing the work. So I called him back, confirmed my interest, and went through the official TEDx application and interview process.

And I was selected.

It would've been easy to second-guess myself. Part of me still felt like an imposter. But I paused and reminded myself of something I say often to others: if you feel the pull, it's for a reason.

From that moment on, it was go time. I went to work to prepare and deliver the most structured talk of my life. I didn't take the opportunity lightly. I wrote, edited, memorized, practiced, refined, and practiced again. I said affirmations like:

- "Words flow to me easily."

- "I'm confident and calm."

- "I was made for this moment."

- "I have an amazing memory and am great at memorizing."

I used every tool I teach: progressive affirmations, visioning, gratitude-based belief shifting, and massive aligned action.

And when I stepped onto that red dot, I was more than ready.

But here's what I want you to take away:

The TEDx talk didn't happen by accident. The dots connected because I kept saying yes. I pursued aligned opportunities even when I didn't have all the answers. I visualized the outcome, stayed open to the path, and followed the flow, even when I was scared.

And yes, I almost said no. Not because it wasn't meant for me, but because I didn't think it could come that easily.

That's what self-sabotage does. It tells you that good things must be hard-earned. It tries to convince you that success isn't real unless you struggle for it.

But that's not true.

Opportunities don't have to feel forced. When you're aligned with your purpose and vision, and you pursue them with faith and flow, unseen forces begin working on your behalf. People appear. Doors open. The timing works.

So, if you're in pursuit of a dream, stay clear. Stay open. Trust that when the dots begin to connect, it's because you've been moving all along, even if you didn't realize it.

And most of all: don't talk yourself out of your moment because it feels easy. Sometimes, flow is the reward for all the unseen effort that led you there.

The entire process, meeting Erik and Jon at Secret Knock, flying to Scottsdale, delivering that talk, meeting two TEDx speakers, starting my own research, and getting that call just in time, was full of moments that looked like coincidence from the outside. But I don't see them that way.

This is what happens when you align your vision with your actions and trust the unseen forces at work. I didn't chase TEDx. I prepared myself for it. And when the moment came, I had the courage to say yes.

POWER IN THE ZONE: AN ATHLETE'S FLOW

Think about athletes at the peak of their game. Whether it's a football player running a perfect play or a martial artist executing a flawless routine, they often talk about entering "the zone." The zone is that heightened state of focus and flow where everything feels effortless, and they are fully present in the moment. They are executing with precision, yet they're not overthinking each move.

As a martial artist, I experienced this during training and competitions. When I hit the zone, I wasn't forcing my movements or thinking about the outcome. My body and mind were in sync, and I was fully immersed in the present moment. I had a clear goal, but I wasn't stressing about how to get there. I let my training, intention, and focus carry me forward. This is the flow state, and it's where true power lives.

When you combine the clarity of your purpose with this state of flow, you unlock more of your true potential. You're working toward your goals while embodying the energy and confidence that come from knowing you're on the right path.

SHINING YOUR LIGHT:
THE RIPPLE EFFECT OF LIVING IN FLOW

Living in flow not only fuels your own growth, it radiates outward. When you're aligned and energized, your presence becomes contagious. You inspire others simply by being you. You show up with clarity and joy, and people feel it.

This is what I mean when I talk about living audaciously joyful. You don't have to be happy all the time. It's about being real, being present, and allowing your purpose and energy to shine through your actions. When you're in flow, you light the way for others, sometimes without even realizing it. You become the kind of person who makes others believe in what's possible for themselves.

LOOKING AHEAD: LETTING GO & MAKING SPACE

Flow invites you to move with purpose, and it also invites you to release control. Just as important as action is the ability to let go of pressure, of perfection, and of outcomes you can't control. In the next chapter, we'll explore how the practices of detachment and forgiveness help you stay in flow, create space for peace, and open the door to even greater fulfillment.

CHAPTER 7

THE ART OF LETTING GO

THE COURAGE OF DETACHMENT & FORGIVENESS

A concept I now live by was shared by Dr. Wayne Dyer, who said, "Be open to everything and attached to nothing." At first glance, detachment may seem like it requires a disconnection from life, from goals, and from our dreams. But detachment is not about withdrawing or not caring. It's releasing our grip on the outcome while still pursuing our goals with intention and passion. Detachment allows us to live with a sense of flow, rooted in the knowledge that we are doing our best without being obsessed with controlling every detail.

This chapter will guide you through understanding detachment, letting go, and the transformative power of forgiveness. Finding peace in life's uncertainties while remaining committed to your purpose.

DETACHMENT: THE FREEDOM IN
LETTING GO OF CONTROL

Being detached does not mean lacking ambition, drive, or passion. In fact, detachment and commitment can coexist. You can keep your dreams and release the attachment to how and when those dreams will come to pass. When we're attached to a specific outcome, we create a sense of lack and fear, fear that we won't succeed, fear that we aren't enough until we achieve the goal. This creates a pressure-filled, forceful energy that blocks joy and prevents us from truly experiencing the process of life.

Detachment is about stepping back, loosening your emotional grip, and letting things unfold naturally. There is a tremendous sense of freedom that comes when we stop trying to control every detail and surrender to life's flow. It feels like a weight has been lifted, as the anxiety of controlling every outcome no longer consumes you. Instead, you learn to trust the process and trust yourself.

One of the most profound aspects of detachment is how it allows you to remain deeply engaged in your goals and actions while also recognizing that you cannot control every factor. As a result, you experience a sense of peace, even as you continue to take meaningful, purposeful actions toward your vision.

EMBRACING LIFE AS IT UNFOLDS

An example of this concept comes from Michael A. Singer's *Surrender Experiment*, in which Singer describes how he chose to surrender his life to whatever came his way, rather than resisting or trying to control the circumstances around him. By allowing life to unfold naturally and trusting that the right opportunities would appear, he found a sense of inner freedom and peace that he had never experienced before. This doesn't mean he stopped working or striving for success; on the contrary, he found that when he stopped resisting life and let go of control, things began to flow more easily, often in ways he never could have planned.

This philosophy of surrender can be applied to our own lives, especially when we feel the pressure to control every step of our journey. When we loosen our grip on the outcomes and trust that life is unfolding exactly as it should, we open ourselves up to opportunities we may have missed in our relentless pursuit of control. Detachment allows us to flow with life, moving forward with purpose and intention but without the burden of anxiety.

HOW DETACHMENT FEELS

Detachment is not a passive process; it requires conscious effort and emotional awareness. When you practice detachment, you experience an energy shift. It feels like a release of tension, a quieting of the mind, and a softening of your emotional state. Imagine feeling fully engaged in your work or your relationships, but without the constant mental chatter of "What if this doesn't work out?" or "What if I'm not good enough?"

Instead, you replace that anxiety with a sense of trust, trust in yourself, trust in the process, trust in a higher power, and trust in the natural flow of life. This emotional release brings a sense of calm and freedom. You begin to move through life with more ease and confidence, knowing that you're doing your best and that whatever happens will ultimately serve your highest good.

There were seasons in my life when I held on too tightly, whether to a business, an identity, or an outcome, and it left me emotionally drained and questioning everything. I'll share one of those stories a little later in this chapter, but first, let's explore how detachment actually frees you to lead and live with more peace and clarity.

DETACHMENT AS FREEDOM FROM EMOTIONAL EXHAUSTION

The world tends to glorify hustle and constant striving, and detachment offers a way to pursue your goals without sacrificing your emotional well-being. When you release attachment to outcomes, you reduce the emotional rollercoaster that comes from being overly invested in things that may be beyond your control. This means you care deeply enough about yourself and your goals to allow them to unfold without the weight of fear or perfectionism.

Practicing detachment also prevents burnout. So much of our stress comes from the emotional energy we waste worrying about things we can't control, how long it will take to achieve success, whether others will approve of our efforts, or whether we'll encounter setbacks along the way. Detachment frees you from this endless cycle of worry and allows you to direct your emotional energy where it truly matters: on the actions and choices that align with your values and purpose.

Detachment might sound a bit naïve to some, like you're just supposed to float through life, unaffected. But it's not about tuning out; it's about tuning in more deeply. When you're no longer controlled by fear or pressure, you're free to access a steadier kind of joy. Not the fleeting high of everything going your way, but the grounded joy of knowing you're aligned with what matters. It's bold, it's peaceful, and it's powerful.

By letting go of the need to control, you create space for more joy, peace, and trust in your life. You can then pursue your goals with clarity, commitment, and a sense of freedom that isn't tied to the outcome.

COMMITMENT VS. ATTACHMENT: THE KEY DIFFERENCE

Commitment is about intention and discipline toward a goal that aligns with your purpose. When you're committed, you act from a place of passion, belief, and love. You trust the process and allow your actions to be driven by purpose, not fear. In contrast, attachment is tied to the outcome. It creates a sense of desperation, making you feel like nothing is good enough until that one thing happens.

Imagine an athlete in the zone, completely focused, moving with precision and purpose. They're committed to winning, but they aren't obsessing over it. They're present in the moment, doing their best, and that's what allows them to perform at their peak. This is flow, and it's the opposite of forcing or pushing for an outcome out of fear or lack.

LETTING GO: TRUSTING THE PROCESS & YOURSELF

Letting go does not mean giving up; it means releasing your grip on the things you can't control. When I was diagnosed with MS at twenty-one, I had no control over what was happening in my body. At first, it was terrifying. But very quickly, I learned that I could control how I responded to it. I chose to let go of the fear and trust in my ability to take care of myself and chart a new path. Letting go allowed me to find my strength and move forward without the weight of fear.

But let me be clear, I'm not perfect at this. It's an ongoing journey, and I continue to get better at it. There are areas of my life where it's become much easier over time, especially as I've been intentional about this practice in the past ten years. Still, there are moments when I slip back into fear, worry, or attachment. The difference now is that I recognize how it feels. I can feel it in my body, in my heart, and I've learned to take a breath, acknowledge it, and then choose a different feeling.

This process is normal and expected, and it's okay to experience moments of resistance. The key is not to resist the resistance but to be open to the journey, knowing that it's all part of the process of growth and detachment.

And this, too, is part of living audaciously joyful, because you choose to meet life with openness even when things don't seem easy. Joy becomes a quiet confidence. Not a denial of hard things, but a willingness to stay connected to what's good, even as you let go of what's heavy.

FORGIVENESS: FREEING YOURSELF, NOT THE OTHER PERSON

Forgiveness is often misunderstood. Some believe that to forgive means to condone the actions of those who have hurt us. But that's not the case. Forgiveness is not about saying what happened was okay; it's about releasing the hold that pain has on your life. So, you can free yourself from the negative emotions that keep you stuck.

A friend of mine went through a difficult time when she found out her husband had been unfaithful. Understandably, she was devastated, and for years she held on to her anger, resentment, and pain. It affected every area of her life, including her confidence, self-esteem, and ability to move forward. It wasn't until she began the process of forgiveness that she started to heal. Forgiving him wasn't about excusing his actions; it was about freeing herself from the emotional prison she had been living in.

Back in Chapter 3, I shared the story of being called "elephant ears" in fourth grade because my ears stuck out, a moment that profoundly shaped how I saw myself and led to personal shame. Looking back, I can see that his comment was a way of coping with his own anger at the time. It doesn't excuse the hurt it caused, but I've come to forgive him, and in doing so, I freed myself too.

Similarly, self-forgiveness is crucial for inner peace. Many of us hold onto guilt or shame for mistakes we've made or things we've failed to do. Just as forgiving others is a path to freedom, so is forgiving yourself. You must recognize that you were doing the best you could with what you knew at the time.

I often tell my clients, "You are enough, and you are always growing." This is where the "and" instead of "but" comes into play. You can accept yourself fully as you are *and* strive for growth. It's not one or the other, it's both. Forgiving yourself allows you to release the weight of past mistakes while creating space for new possibilities.

WHEN HOLDING IT ALL TOGETHER BECOMES TOO HEAVY

There was a season in my life when I was doing everything I could to make my health food store successful. I had poured my heart, savings, and years of passion into it. On paper, I was combining my business background with my deep love for nutrition and wellness, helping people live healthier lives while building a business that aligned with my purpose.

But behind the scenes, it was becoming harder and harder to keep the business afloat. Sales had slowed, overhead was rising, my values had shifted after my son was born, and the emotional weight of holding it all together was heavy. I was managing the operations, and I was also trying to hold space for my team, for our customers, for our brand, and for the vision I had clung to since the beginning. I told myself I had to stay strong. I had to figure it out. I had to be the one who made it work.

Looking back, I can see how perfectionism was driving me: I measured my worth by my ability to solve every problem, lead perfectly, and keep things together no matter what. I carried the pressure silently. I didn't want to burden anyone. But deep down, I was exhausted.

Eventually, with my husband's guidance and support, I reached the point where I knew I needed to sell the store. It was one of the hardest decisions I've ever made. I remember walking into a franchise real estate agent's office, hoping they'd see the potential I still believed was there. I explained everything I had built, our loyal customer base, the beautiful storefront, the wellness professionals we had brought in, and the heart behind the work.

He listened, looked through the numbers, and then, with a quiet honesty, he said something I'll never forget:

"You'd have to pay someone to take this business off your hands."

That sentence cut through every layer of optimism I was still clinging to. It wasn't cruel, it was just real. But in that moment, I felt deeply ashamed. Embarrassed. Like all the hard work, sacrifice, and hope I had poured into that store, was being labeled worthless in a single sentence.

If I wasn't kind to myself, the thoughts that came up could have been cruel. Today, I would never use language like that toward myself or anyone else. But in that moment, the inner critic was loud. *How could I let this happen? How did I not see it sooner? What does this say about me?*

It was one of the lowest moments of my entrepreneurial life. I questioned everything, my decisions, my leadership, my identity. If this business had failed, did that mean I was a failure?

And yet, looking back now, I see how much that moment taught me. It stripped away the ego. It forced me to look at who I was without the title, the storefront, or the illusion of success. And what I found underneath was something deeper: resilience, humility, and a new kind of strength. That store didn't define me. But what I learned in its unraveling did.

And honestly, if I hadn't done the deep work I've done over the past decade, work that's in this very book, I don't know if I'd be able to write about it now with this much clarity and compassion.

I've learned to forgive myself for staying in it too long, for trying to do it all, for striving to be perfect, for measuring success by external metrics instead of emotional truth. I've forgiven myself for the silent burdens I carried and for judging myself so harshly in the process. And more than that, I've come to see that this unraveling wasn't a failure, it was a turning point. It cracked me open in a way that allowed something far more aligned to emerge.

If you're a leader, a business owner, a parent, or anyone who's carried silent shame over something that didn't go as planned, I want you to hear this: you're not alone. You are not your results. And sometimes, what feels like the end is actually the turning point.

I hope my story gives you permission to breathe a little deeper, and maybe even extend the same compassion to yourself that you'd offer someone else in your shoes. Because before we can fully let go and move forward, we often have to make peace with who we were when we were just trying our best.

MOVING FORWARD WITH LIGHTNESS & GRACE

Letting go of control, past mistakes, or the need to have it all figured out makes room for something softer, more spacious. It clears the way for lightness. And with lightness comes joy.

You don't have to carry every burden to be strong. In fact, some of your greatest strength will come when you release the weight you were never meant to hold.

As we move into the next chapter, we'll look at how kindness, especially when rooted in gratitude, can help you not only feel more joyful but also *become* someone who spreads that joy to others. When you're free on the inside, it shows on the outside.

CHAPTER 8

BECOMING ENOUGH

A JOURNEY THROUGH GRATITUDE: THE JOURNEY FROM NOT-ENOUGHNESS TO ALWAYS ENOUGH

Growing up, I was often the new kid. My family moved frequently, which meant I was constantly navigating new schools, new neighborhoods, and new social circles. Each move brought a fresh start, but also a familiar challenge: the need to fit in.

As a child, I learned to be agreeable, to not rock the boat, to be pleasant but not too loud, to be fun but not too different. I believed that if I could just be the right version of myself, I would be accepted. I was a generally happy and positive child, but beneath that exterior was a lingering feeling of not being quite enough.

That feeling followed me into high school. I had close friends, and I was involved in activities, clubs, and leadership roles. Outwardly, things looked good. But inwardly, I still had that quiet pressure: don't mess this up. Don't be annoying. Don't be too much. Make sure you're helpful, smart, funny, but not in a way that stands out *too* much. I would overanalyze conversations, worry about whether I'd said the wrong thing, and quietly try to manage how I was perceived. I never would've said I was insecure; I didn't even fully realize it at the time. But I was living through the lens of proving I was enough.

It continued into university. I made friends, got good grades, enjoyed the freedom of living on my own, but the feeling remained. That low hum in the background made me wonder if I was being judged, if I needed to try harder, if other people were more naturally accepted than I was.

Then came my corporate career. I had great working relationships. I worked hard, got promoted, and led teams. I loved the work I did and the people I worked with. I was respected and recognized. From the outside, there was no reason to think I didn't belong.

But that same quiet belief followed me in. The belief that I needed to prove myself to earn a seat at the table. That maybe I wasn't *quite* as good as others. That if I said or did the wrong thing, I'd lose respect. No one around me would have guessed it, because it wasn't about how I looked or sounded. It was about how I *felt*.

When I left the corporate world and became an entrepreneur, that belief didn't disappear. I started going to networking events to promote my health store, and once again, that familiar feeling surfaced. Everyone else seemed so confident, so established. I looked polished and prepared on the outside, but inside, I often felt like the outsider in the room, hoping no one would realize I didn't quite feel like I belonged.

As the years went by, I naturally started to recognize that I didn't have to care quite so much what other people thought. It wasn't as loud anymore, but it still lingered. I started to understand that it wasn't truth, it was a habit. A deeply ingrained identity I had worn for so long, I hadn't realized it was optional.

The turning point began when I was introduced to Bob Proctor's teachings and first explored the power of the mind. I started to learn how beliefs shape identity and how we often unconsciously live out stories that no longer serve us. And when we believe the story, then our mind continues to show us examples to prove that belief is true—even when it isn't. My deepest transformation happened when I began working with Tony Child through the GratiShift™ program.

It was there that I was reintroduced to gratitude, not only as a journal prompt or a morning routine, but as a powerful tool to shift identity, to truly live and be grateful. Gratitude at the deepest level helped me stop seeing myself, others, and the world through the lens of lack. It helped me see what was *already* working. It helped me realize that I didn't have to earn worthiness. I already had it. I didn't have to prove I belonged. I *do* belong. I didn't have to be more or less to be accepted. I am already enough.

This gratitude practice and shift not only made me feel better, it changed how I *saw* my circumstances, the people in my life and especially how I saw myself. It changed my identity.

It helped me rewrite the silent story I'd been carrying since childhood. The one that said "You're only safe if you shrink." Gratitude helped me grow into the version of myself that no longer needed to hide. And that shift changed the way I led, the way I connected with others, and the way I viewed my purpose.

That is the power of deep gratitude: it restores truth. It dissolves false identities. And it returns us to the knowing that we are, and always have been, enough.

And here's what matters just as much: I continue to practice gratitude at this depth every single day. More than writing a list or thinking a positive thought. I am intentionally living from a place of appreciation. Seeing the good in myself and others. Feeling thankful for the small and the significant. Overflowing that emotion into generosity and presence. It's not something I did once and arrived. It's something I *choose* again and again.

Like any transformation, I'm not perfect at it. I don't live in a constant state of bliss or total confidence. There are still moments, rare and quiet now, when that old pattern tries to sneak in. But the difference is, it's softer. It doesn't grab hold. I notice it. I meet it with curiosity, not judgment. And I shift gently back into truth. That's the work. Not to never fall, but to fall less often, less hard, and get back up with kindness.

That's what I hope for you, too. Not a perfect life, but a grounded one. One where gratitude becomes your anchor. Where the voice of not-enoughness grows quieter. And the truth of who you are becomes the one that speaks the loudest.

GRATITUDE AS A NEW LENS

Gratitude isn't a list. It's a lens.

It's the shift from mentally checking off what's good to *feeling* what's already working. It's the difference between saying, "I should be thankful," and truly embodying, "I am thankful."

As I write this chapter, I'm sitting by the lake. The water is calm, the breeze is light, and the beauty surrounding me is quiet and undeniable. It reminds me how easy it is to miss the abundance that's all around us, unless we're not only looking for it, but *feeling* it. Gratitude lives in those small, sacred moments of awareness.

That's the real power: intentionally choosing to see through a lens of appreciation, even, and especially, when things are hard. When life feels uncertain. When challenges arise.

Gratitude means anchoring yourself in what's good. What's working. What's true. Not pretending that everything is perfect.

It can be as simple as noticing the way the clouds look different every day, or recognizing the comfort of clean water and a warm meal. I used to invite my son when he was little to pay attention to the sky, because no two cloud formations are ever the same. At first, he didn't get it. But over time, he began to notice. Now, he's the one pointing out the sky to me. That's gratitude in motion. That's presence.

It also extends to the people in your life. Noticing the specific moments of care, effort, and connection, the small, often invisible things that build love and trust. Gratitude, when specific, becomes a magnifier of meaning.

It also transforms how you move through the everyday.

You don't *have to* pay your bills, you *get to*. You don't *need to* cook dinner, you *get to* nourish yourself and those you love. You don't *have to* take a break, you *get to* honor your energy.

This mindset shift is about reclaiming the frequency of abundance. When you slow down, become present, and choose to see what's already enough, you create space for more. This is how gratitude shifts your identity.

It teaches you to stop seeking worth from the outside and start recognizing it from within. It changes how you see yourself, others, and the world around you. It becomes a lens of *enoughness*. A way of living in presence and fullness, without needing anything to be perfect.

A STORY OF UNEXPECTED GRATITUDE: FINDING GIFTS IN ADVERSITY

About twenty years ago, a friend of mine had a younger sister who went through an unimaginable experience. His sister was eighteen at the time, but due to a mild mental disability, her mental capacity was closer to that of a ten-year-old. Despite her kind and friendly nature, she often faced bullying because her behavior didn't match her physical appearance. People didn't understand her, and it was sometimes a challenging reality for her and her family.

Then, doctors discovered a large brain tumor. She underwent surgery to remove it, and while the operation was successful, she woke up to a devastating outcome: she had lost her sight. She went from having 20/20 vision to complete darkness overnight. Although the doctors had assured the family that blindness was a rare side effect, she was part of the unfortunate 1%.

For her and her family, this was a tragic loss. Going from full vision to complete blindness was unimaginable, and the emotional toll was immense. However, after months of rehabilitation and adjustment, something unexpected happened. She regained her independence with the help of a walking cane, and eventually a service dog, and she could once again navigate the world on her own. Then, about six months after the surgery, she said something that stunned us:

"Going blind was one of the greatest gifts that ever happened to me."

She explained that before losing her sight, people couldn't see her mental disability, and they often treated her poorly because she didn't act "normally" for her age. But once she became visibly blind, people started treating her with kindness and respect. Strangers offered her help, gave up their seats for her, and treated her with the dignity she had always longed for.

Her blindness made her disability visible to the world, and it changed how people interacted with her. She found a deep sense of gratitude for the kindness and compassion she now received, a gift she never could have imagined.

This story is a powerful reminder that even in the darkest of circumstances, there is room for gratitude. Sometimes, the most unexpected situations bring about the greatest gifts, and our ability to shift our perspective can lead us to see these blessings in disguise.

GRATITUDE: THE ABILITY TO RECEIVE

Gratitude is also the state of receiving. When we practice gratitude, we align ourselves with the abundance that already exists in our lives. There's a quote I've always loved: "The secret to having it all is knowing you already do." This speaks to the essence of gratitude, being thankful for what you have, and recognizing that you're *worthy* of it. Right now. As you are. To me, it means seeing from a state of wholeness rather than lack.

And interestingly, that opens the door to more. Because you are in a state of flow.

Many people, especially those who are generous by nature, find receiving uncomfortable. They give and give, sometimes to the point of depletion, but struggle to accept a compliment, a helping hand, or even a moment of rest. They've learned to equate giving with value and receiving with weakness or selfishness.

But if you think about it, for generosity to exist, someone has to be willing to receive. It's a full circle. And when we anchor into gratitude, we naturally begin to soften that resistance. We remember that we don't have to earn goodness. We're allowed to receive it.

Living in a state of gratitude helps us stop trying to prove we're enough and start allowing ourselves to experience the abundance that was already there.

Gratitude, kindness, and unconditional love all operate on a similar frequency. According to David R. Hawkins' consciousness scale, gratitude and love sit right beside each other at the highest levels of vibration. When you live in a state of gratitude, you naturally open yourself up to experience and share unconditional love.

This love extends not only to your family members, but to everyone around you. And it starts early. One of the most powerful places we see this play out is in how we raise and treat children. I'll share more on that a bit later in this chapter.

THE COURAGE OF TRUE KINDNESS

Kindness and gratitude are also intertwined. When you believe you are enough and that there is enough, kindness flows naturally. Not as a performance, not out of obligation, but as an overflow of how you see yourself and the world.

And true kindness requires courage. It is about caring deeply, even when that care means doing something uncomfortable. Like telling someone they have broccoli in their teeth before a meeting. Or setting a boundary with love. Or choosing not to react when you're hurt, but instead responding with grace.

Several years ago, when I worked in corporate, I was on a business trip with my boss, Dawson Marshall. I was reading a book about kindness on the flight, and Dawson gently asked me, "Why would someone as kind as you need to read a book about kindness?" That question made me stop and reflect. Why *was* I reading it? I know I am a genuinely nice person. But I also believe we can always grow. Kindness isn't something you master; it's something you continually deepen.

136

True kindness means giving without expectation. Offering your time, energy, and love freely, not to prove anything, but because you're already full. Because you're grounded in enoughness.

Whether it's a smile to someone who's feeling down or extending a hand to a stranger, the *heart* behind the act is what matters most. Kindness becomes less about the action and more about the *energy* it's rooted in. And when that energy comes from a place of gratitude and worth, it has the power to ripple further than we can imagine.

THE POWER OF SILENCE:
KINDNESS IN LETTING GO

Kindness isn't always about what you say or do, it's often about what you choose not to say or do. In many cases, the kindest thing you can do is to let something go or choose silence. Have you ever found yourself in the middle of an argument, only to realize you've forgotten what you were even fighting about? Often, we react in the heat of the moment, saying things we don't mean or engaging in conflict that doesn't serve anyone.

True kindness sometimes means not picking a fight, even when you feel frustrated. It means accepting the present moment for what it is, understanding that reality doesn't always align with your expectations, but fighting it won't change it. Instead, kindness can be found in surrendering to the present while still holding space for creating a better future.

By letting go of the need to be right or to have the last word, you give both yourself and the other person the gift of peace. Kindness is found in the ability to recognize when words or actions will only escalate a situation and choosing instead to allow space for understanding and calm to take over. It's the act of releasing resentment, of choosing compassion over conflict, and of trusting that silence or non-action can be just as powerful as any spoken word.

That said, there are times when setting healthy boundaries is equally an act of kindness. If a situation is unhealthy or unsafe, kindness might mean creating distance or asserting your needs. Boundaries protect your well-being while allowing you to show up more fully in your relationships, knowing when to step back and when to engage with love and respect.

Kindness is also about accepting that not everything needs to be fixed right away. Some situations simply need time and space to resolve themselves, and by offering that space, you allow for healing and growth in a way that no argument or action could achieve. Letting something go in the present moment can be an act of generosity and love, both for yourself and for those around you.

UNCONDITIONAL LOVE:
THE FOUNDATION OF TRUE GENEROSITY

True kindness and generosity are often linked to unconditional love, the kind of love that is not dependent on what someone else does or doesn't do. This is particularly impactful in the way we raise and treat children. As a parent or caregiver, when you are in a state of gratitude and kindness, you are more likely to extend unconditional love to your child, teaching them that they are loved simply because they exist, not because of what they do.

Unconditional love means accepting and caring for others without placing conditions on that love. It's the kind of love that says, "I love you whether you succeed or fail, whether you make the right choice or not." When a child feels this kind of love, it sets the foundation for their self-esteem and their beliefs about themselves and the world. If a child feels that love is conditional, they may grow up thinking they must constantly earn love through their actions or accomplishments.

This isn't to say that we don't recognize the child when they achieve something and congratulate them and say, "You should be proud of yourself!" This isn't to say you can't validate their disappointment when something doesn't go as they hoped. It simply means that our love for them is not a reflection of outside conditions. "I love you, and I didn't like that behavior." "I love you, you are lovable, worthy of love, and an amazing person, even when you take actions that don't serve you. You are still worthy of love and can learn and grow."

When I was working in corporate in Toronto, Canada, during a particularly stressful time, I would go to a restorative yoga class. At one of the classes, during savasana at the end, the time when all the yoga students are lying down on our backs, eyes closed, resting, the yoga instructor read a poem out loud for us that impacted me so deeply that I still remember it and think of it often twenty years later. Mother Teresa's famous poem, *"Anyway,"* beautifully captures this essence of giving with love:

> *"People are often unreasonable, illogical and self-centered; Forgive them anyway.*
>
> *If you are kind, people may accuse you of selfish, ulterior motives;*
> *Be kind anyway.*
>
> *If you are successful, you will win some false friends and some true enemies;*
> *Succeed anyway.*
>
> *If you are honest and frank, people may cheat you;*
> *Be honest and frank anyway.*
>
> *What you spend years building, someone could destroy overnight;*
> *Build anyway.*
> *If you find serenity and happiness, they may be jealous;*
> *Be happy anyway.*
>
> *The good you do today, people will often forget tomorrow;*
> *Do good anyway.*

Give the world the best you have, and it may never be enough;
Give the world the best you've got anyway.

You see, in the final analysis, it is between you and your God;
It was never between you and them anyway."

– Mother Theresa

This poem is a powerful reminder that kindness and generosity are about who you are, not about how others respond. You give and love because it's who you are, not because of the recognition or reward that might come back to you. It's this pure form of kindness that creates true abundance in the world.

A PRACTICE YOU CAN BEGIN RIGHT NOW

You can begin shifting your entire life through gratitude and kindness starting today.

Right now.

Pause. Close your eyes for a moment and ask yourself: what are three things you're thankful for? They can be big or small, a person, a moment, a smile, the way the sunlight touches the trees outside your window.

Now feel it. Don't just list the items, pause and let yourself truly experience the emotion of gratitude. Let it settle in your body like warmth. Let it expand.

And from that place of appreciation, take one small, generous action. Send a kind message to someone. Do something thoughtful without expecting recognition. Smile at a stranger. Or be kind to yourself, truly kind. Drink a glass of water and thank your body. Forgive yourself for something. Rest, if that's what you need.

Gratitude, kindness, generosity, and self-compassion are practical tools. They shift how we see, how we feel, and who we believe ourselves to be. This is how we return to the truth.

You are enough. The world is full of goodness. And there is more than enough to go around.

Let yourself see it. Let yourself feel it. Let yourself become it.

That's the shift. As Tony Child defines it, the GratiShift™. And it's the art of living audaciously joyful.

CHAPTER 9

THE POWER OF PLAY

....

REDISCOVERING YOUR
CHILD-LIKE JOY

Imagine for a moment stepping into the life of your inner child. Remember those moments of pure, unfiltered joy… running through a sprinkler on a hot summer day, rolling down a grassy hill without a care, or laughing so hard your stomach hurt. There was no to-do list, no pressure to be productive. It was just you and the freedom of the moment, fully immersed in play.

Play is a powerful way to release stress, spark creativity, and connect with others on a deeper level. As adults, we often underestimate the value of play, and yet it is one of the most effective ways to recharge our minds, bodies, and spirits.

THE INNER BATTLE: LETTING GO TO PLAY

If you're like me, the logical, driven part of your mind might resist the idea of setting aside time for play. "I should be doing something productive," that inner voice might say. "There are chores to do, emails to answer, or goals to meet." That resistance is normal. As adults, we've been conditioned to prioritize productivity and responsibility above all else.

The interesting thing is that play is not the opposite of productivity; it's the gateway to creativity and connection. When you allow yourself to play, you unlock a different state of being. You tap into presence, flow, and a sense of freedom that carries over into other areas of your life.

WHY PLAY MATTERS

Play is a vital part of our well-being as adults. Studies have shown that incorporating play into your life can reduce stress, boost creativity, and improve relationships. Laughter, movement, and shared moments of fun release endorphins, improve mental clarity, and create stronger bonds with others.

For me, play often happens with my ten-year-old son. Whether we're sledding down a snowy hill, building LEGO creations, or jumping in the pool, those moments of play bring lightness and connection to our lives. But I'll admit, sometimes it's a struggle to let go of my adult responsibilities and step into that world of play. My inner voice often tells me I should be working on my business or tackling some household chores.

But every time I choose play, I'm reminded of its power. It changes my energy, sparks creativity, and brings more joy into my day. It's a reminder that life is not about doing, it's about being. We aren't "human-doings," we are "human-beings."

PLAY AS A GATEWAY TO JOY & CREATIVITY

One of my favorite forms of play as an adult is through CrossFit. While it's a workout, it also reminds me of being a child, especially when I practice gymnastics-style movements like handstands or hanging from the high rings. At first, I was terrified to try a handstand again—I hadn't done one since I was a kid! But I pushed through the fear, and now it feels powerful and fun.

When my son joins me at CrossFit, it becomes an even greater experience. We share moments of connection, strength, and laughter, and I'm reminded of how important it is to step out of our comfort zones and embrace play in all its forms.

Play can look different for everyone. It might be a team sport, dancing in your living room, painting, or even a spontaneous snowball fight. What matters is that it brings you joy and lets you express yourself freely.

SINGING, LAUGHING, & LETTING LOOSE

I've realized that one of the most important ways I stay connected to my childlike spirit is by letting myself be silly. For me, that often shows up when I'm driving, alone, with my son, or even with someone else in the car who probably thinks I'm a little quirky. I'll turn up the music, sing along, bounce to the beat, and dance in my seat. There's something freeing about letting the music take over and not worrying about who's watching. That's what a childlike spirit feels like: freedom.

Another favorite? Laughing out loud. I have a few friends who have the most contagious laughs, and sometimes I start laughing not even at whatever they are laughing at, but simply because their laugh is so joyful. You probably have someone like that in your life, too; just being around them brings out your giggles. You're probably smiling just thinking about it. Laughter, especially shared laughter, is one of the fastest ways to return to joy.

LAUGHING AT YOURSELF

Some of the best laughter comes from not taking ourselves so seriously. I had one moment in particular that still makes me laugh and blush when I remember it.

It was over a decade ago, and I was in a yoga class. The room was quiet, with peaceful music playing and the instructor's soft voice guiding us. We transitioned into the downward dog position, and as I bent deeply into the position... I accidentally farted. It echoed slightly in the otherwise silent room. There was no mistaking the sound.

At first, I was mortified. But then I started laughing. The teacher laughed. The class laughed. And you know what? It was fine. That memory is mostly funny now, not embarrassing. It taught me something: when you can laugh at yourself, life becomes lighter. Mistakes become moments of connection. Vulnerability becomes a bridge to joy.

LAUGHTER RUNS IN THE FAMILY

Laughter has always been a big part of my family, especially with my two younger sisters. Even now, as adults, we still find ourselves laughing hysterically over random things, laughing at each other, with each other, or at something that makes no sense at all. It's one of our favorite forms of connection. And even now that we live farther apart, it's a way we stay close. We actually share laughs almost daily in our group chat.

Our dad has always been someone who makes people laugh, often without even trying. One morning when we were kids, he came downstairs with only half his mustache shaved off and didn't say a word. Eventually, we noticed and burst out laughing. As the morning went on, he had forgotten he had done it, and later went to work like that! It's still one of our funniest family stories. That image lives on as a symbol of playfulness, ridiculousness, and not taking life too seriously.

This is one of the most significant gifts of play: lightness. The childlike part of you is light, forgiving, and quick to return to joy. When something goes wrong, kids might cry or get upset, but then, just minutes later, they're back to playing. They don't hold grudges the way adults do. They forgive easily, reconnect quickly, and move forward with open hearts.

I see this all the time with my son and his friends. One minute, they're arguing or upset, and the next, they're inventing a new game together, laughing like nothing ever happened. It's not that kids don't feel pain; it's that they don't hold on to it the same way we do. They live in the moment. We can learn from that.

WHEN PLAY FEELS HARD

For some people, tapping into play might feel awkward or even painful. Not everyone had a carefree childhood. Some people grew up too fast, felt unsafe being silly, or were taught that being playful was immature or irresponsible. If play was met with criticism or rejection, it makes sense that it may not come naturally now.

You are not broken if play feels hard.

My business partner, Tony, often shares that he didn't experience much play growing up. His mom was in a wheelchair, his dad worked long hours, and Tony stepped into a caregiver role at a very young age. Cooking, cleaning, taking on responsibility. For him, play was something that had to be relearned as an adult.

And he's doing just that. As an adult, rediscovering the art of play can be healing. It's something he chooses consciously.

He teaches his nervous system that it's okay to relax. That it's okay to have fun.

If that's you too, let this be your permission slip: play doesn't have to be loud or wild. It can be gentle. It can start small. A moment of laughter. A curious "what if." A silly dance in the kitchen with your kids. Even a smile at your own reflection.

Let play meet you where you are.

PRESENCE: THE KEY TO PLAY

One of the greatest gifts of play is that it brings you into the present moment. When you're fully engaged in play, whether it's a game with your child, a creative project, or a lighthearted conversation, you're not worrying about the past or future. You're simply present.

And if you struggle to find joy in play, focus on the joy it brings to others. When I play with my son or my nieces and nephews, part of the fun is seeing their joy. Their joy is contagious and reminds me why play is essential.

YOU WERE BORN TO PLAY

Here's a truth we forget as we grow older: you were born with creativity, joy, and playfulness. These qualities are your birthright. Life experiences may have taught you to suppress them, but they're still inside you.

Think back to a moment when you felt carefree and joyful, even if it's faint. That wonder and lightness are still available to you. It may take practice to reconnect with it, but it's worth the effort.

PRACTICAL WAYS TO INCORPORATE PLAY

If you're ready to invite more play into your life, here are a few ways to start:

- **Schedule playtime:** Just as you schedule meetings or workouts, block off time for play—even ten minutes counts.

- **Try something new:** Novelty makes play even more fun—karaoke, paddleboarding, finger painting, etc.

- **Be silly on purpose:** Let go of looking cool. Dance badly. Make goofy faces. Say yes to ridiculousness.

- **Play with others:** Whether it's with your kids, friends, or even strangers at a community event, play is often more fun when shared.

THE LIGHTNESS OF BEING

Play isn't a luxury, it's not childish, it's not something you earn only after the work is done. It's a return to joy and a return to presence. A return to your whole self.

It helps you create memories, heal old stories, and live in the moment. And most of all, it makes life feel worth living.

There's a book I was introduced to years ago called *Don't Sweat the Small Stuff... and It's All Small Stuff.* The title stuck with me. At the time, it felt radical. *What do you mean it's all small stuff?* But I've come to understand that most of what weighs us down daily isn't the serious stuff. It's the pressure, the performance, the expectations. Play cuts through that. Laughter breaks it open.

One of my favorite quotes on this is from Steve Harvey, who said, "Laugh every chance you get. Even if it ain't funny, just bust out laughing. Ha! Ha! Ha!" If you've ever heard his laugh, you know it's contagious. That kind of energy is what this world needs more of.

So, let that be your invitation. Laugh every chance you get, even if it ain't funny.

Sing in the car. Laugh with your sisters. Fart in yoga. Be silly. Be light. Let your childlike spirit have space again. You were born to play.

And in the next chapter, we'll talk about another core pillar of living audaciously joyful, how you fuel your body and move your energy. Because how you eat, move, and nourish yourself affects how much joy you can access in the first place.

Let's keep going. Boldly. Joyfully. Together.

CHAPTER 10

FUELING A JOYFUL LIFE

REAL TALK ON NUTRITION & MOVEMENT

When it comes to health, what you put in your body can change everything from how you feel physically to how you think and process emotions. Nutrition is the foundation for well-being, energy, and long-term vitality. However, no two people are exactly the same when it comes to what their bodies need. Whether you're managing a chronic condition or simply aiming for optimal health, the key lies in personalized nutrition, fitness, and an understanding of how these elements fuel both your body and mind.

Having owned a health food store for three years and worked alongside a variety of natural health practitioners, from nutritionists and naturopaths to personal trainers and osteopaths, I've seen firsthand how personalized nutrition and fitness can positively impact people's lives. While I'm no longer practicing as a Nutritional Practitioner or Personal

Trainer, I hold a certification in both nutrition and personal training, and I've spent years researching how food and fitness affect the body and mind. Through these experiences, I've developed deep insights into the connection between what we eat, how we move, and how we ultimately feel.

This chapter will focus on how nutrition and fitness come together to create long-term health and well-being. We'll explore the gut-brain connection, how mindset influences your eating habits, and why it's essential to develop a sustainable approach to nutrition and exercise that works for your unique body and goals.

THE POWER OF NUTRITION & FITNESS COMBINED

Nutrition is about fueling your body with the right nutrients to optimize mental clarity, emotional balance, and physical performance. What you eat directly impacts your mood, energy levels, and even how you recover from stress or illness. Combined with fitness, these elements become a powerful foundation for long-term well-being.

In my personal journey, the connection between nutrition and fitness became even clearer after my diagnosis with multiple sclerosis (MS). My focus on nutrition and physical health helped me regain strength, manage symptoms, and maintain a balanced, fulfilling life. The foods I chose and the workouts I committed to were about feeling strong and about supporting my brain health, mental clarity, and long-term vitality.

Through the years, I've followed a version of the **Wahls Protocol**, a diet designed to support brain health and reduce inflammation. While I've adapted this protocol to fit my needs over the years, it emphasizes nutrient-dense whole foods, including a high intake of vegetables, essential fatty acids, and lean proteins, and is gluten-free and dairy-free. Dr. Wahls describes her book and protocol as, "How I beat progressive MS using paleo principles and functional medicine." The combination of this diet with regular exercise,including strength training, cardio, and flexibility work, has allowed me to maintain my health and energy, even as I manage a chronic condition, keeping a positive mindset as my foundation.

It's important to note that after about ten years, I did gradually add back into my diet some grains—only gluten-free grains about once per day—and yogurt, once a day or less, which are not components of the official Wahls protocol.

THE GUT-BRAIN CONNECTION: WHY IT MATTERS

One of the most fascinating areas of research in recent years is the **gut-brain connection**. The gut is often referred to as the "second brain" because it contains millions of neurons and communicates directly with the brain. The foods you eat do more than nourish your body; they play a crucial role in your mood, cognitive function, and overall mental health.

When your gut is healthy, you're more likely to experience balanced emotions, mental clarity, and resilience to stress. However, when your gut is irritated, whether due to poor nutrition, stress, or other factors, it can lead to inflammation, mood swings, brain fog, and even anxiety or depression.

For me, managing a chronic condition like MS, gut health becomes even more critical. The gut-brain connection affects everything from immune function to inflammation levels, both of which are key in managing symptoms and supporting overall brain health. By prioritizing gut health through proper nutrition, choosing anti-inflammatory foods, probiotics, and fiber-rich vegetables while potentially removing foods that irritate your gut or working with a health professional to check for food sensitivities, you're feeding your brain and also setting the foundation for long-term physical and emotional well-being.

THE PSYCHOLOGY OF NUTRITION: MINDSET & SELF-IMAGE SHAPE YOUR CHOICES

Understanding nutrition is one part of the equation. Your **mindset** plays an equally important role in how you approach food and fitness. In my experience, helping clients improve their health often meant working on their mindset just as much as their eating habits.

There's a psychological component to nutrition that can't be overlooked. Many people struggle to sustain healthy eating habits because of deep-rooted beliefs about their self-worth, their identity, and their ability to change. They may know what they should be eating, but old habits, emotional eating, or a lack of self-confidence keep them from sticking to their goals.

THE THERMOSTATIC EFFECT:
RESETTING YOUR SELF-IMAGE FOR HEALTH

The thermostatic effect is a powerful analogy when it comes to self-image and nutrition. As Dr. Maxwell Maltz explained in his book, Psycho-Cybernetics, your self-image acts like a thermostat, regulating your behavior in all areas of life—including how you approach your health. If your self-image is set at a "lower" level, you'll unconsciously sabotage your own efforts to improve your diet or fitness. Examples of self-talk at a lower level might include, "I've always been this way," "I can't resist sweets," "This health condition runs in my family," or "I hate the gym." These thoughts reflect a mindset that keeps your thermostat stuck, pulling you back to your default habits, even when you attempt to make healthier changes.

Although these may feel like facts in your reality, they are not permanent truths. To create lasting change, it's crucial to **change the narrative** you tell yourself. This is where **progressive affirmations**, as we discussed in Chapter 4, become a powerful tool for shifting your self-image. Instead of jumping to "I love the gym," when that might feel unbelievable, you can start with a progressive affirmation like, "I am open to finding movement that I enjoy and that benefits my body." Over time, this subtle shift in language can help reframe how you see yourself and your relationship with health.

If you've always believed, "I can't resist sweets," you can start with, "I'm learning to make healthier choices that nourish my body." This progressive affirmation begins the process of rewiring your self-image, moving your thermostat up to a higher level where making healthy choices becomes more natural. As you shift your self-talk, you'll notice your actions begin to align with this new identity, which is the key to long-term, sustainable health.

When your self-image shifts, when you start to see yourself as a healthy, fit person, everything changes. Suddenly, making healthy choices becomes easier because it's aligned with who you believe yourself to be. You no longer have to force yourself to eat well or work out; it becomes a natural extension of your identity.

For me, a key transformation came when people stopped offering me donuts. When I was a kid, my parents and grandparents owned Tim Horton's franchises for a number of years (for those of you not in Canada, Tim Horton's is a coffee shop with locations all across our country and well known for their donuts and coffee). After my MS experience and transition into health, people stopped offering me donuts. It wasn't because I had told them, "I'm not allowed" to eat donuts. It was because I no longer identified with being the type of person who *would* eat a donut. My self-image had shifted so thoroughly that my actions naturally followed suit. It wasn't about forcing myself into willpower mode,it was about aligning my choices with the healthy person I had become, and that person ate a gluten-free and nutritious diet.

It's important to recognize that shifting your self-image is one of the most powerful ways to create lasting change. When you begin to see yourself as a healthy, fit person, even if you're still at the beginning of your journey, your actions naturally start to align with that identity. External results often follow the internal shift.

For example, I had a client who had struggled with maintaining healthy eating habits and exercise for years. No matter how many diets she tried or good intentions she had, she always ended up reverting to her old behaviors, and always had a reason as to why she couldn't stick to it. As we worked together, it became clear that she still saw herself as someone who was "bad" at sticking to healthy habits. She would say things like, "I've never been able to do this," "I don't have time to exercise," "My work is more important," or "I always fail." Her self-image was keeping her locked in a cycle of defeat.

Once we worked on shifting her subconscious mindset, helping her see herself as someone capable of success, someone who *deserved* to be healthy, her actions began to change. She didn't just *try* another diet; she embraced a healthier lifestyle because that's the kind of person she started to believe herself to be. She was willing to put work activities aside in order to get to the gym. She was more easily able to say no to unhealthy food choices when out with friends or peers at restaurants. She truly saw herself as a healthy person.

During this process of self-image transformation, you may need to teach others about the new version of yourself, especially if they've known the "old you" for years. For instance, at the start of my journey, people were still offering me donuts and unhealthy options because they hadn't yet seen me as the healthy person I had become. Over time, as I consistently made choices that reflected my new identity, those offers stopped. People now see me as someone who makes healthy choices, not because I *have to*, but because it's simply who I am. Those of you who know me today know that I'd be the one to bring kale salad or a veggie and hummus tray to a party.

When you begin to ask yourself, "What would a healthy person do?" and shift to identify as that type of person, the answers come easily. You'll find yourself taking the stairs, choosing the salad, or saying no to the donut because it's simply who you are, not out of force.

THE LONG-TERM APPROACH:
WHAT WORKS FOR ME

My own approach to nutrition has evolved over the years. I've followed a variation of the **Wahls Protocol**, which focuses on brain health, anti-inflammatory foods, and high nutrient intake. I've adapted the protocol to fit my needs, and my core principles: lots of vegetables, lean proteins, healthy fats, minimal processed foods and gluten-free remain the foundation of my diet.

Here's a sample of my current daily routine:

- **Breakfast**: I start with a large glass of water with lemon and apple cider vinegar, and then a smoothie loaded with spinach, zucchini, berries, and protein powder (usually plant-based protein). I make sure to get a balance of protein, fiber, and healthy fats to fuel my morning.

- **Lunch**: A big salad with mixed greens, cucumbers, tomatoes, and a protein source like chicken or eggs. I usually make my own balsamic vinaigrette for a light but flavorful dressing and might toss in some walnuts or pumpkin seeds. Plus a gluten-free starch like potatoes or rice.

- **Snack**: Veggies and hummus, nuts, a bowl of Greek yogurt with chia seeds and/or an "energy ball" which includes dark chocolate chip oats, nut butter, chia seeds and honey.

- **Dinner**: A protein like fish or chicken, accompanied by roasted vegetables and sometimes another gluten-free starch like sweet potatoes or rice. I aim for a colorful variety of vegetables to ensure I'm getting a broad spectrum of nutrients.

- **Optional Snack**: Possibly another protein shake or Greek yogurt with berries if dinner was early or if it's post-evening workout.

- **Supplements**: Over the years, I've consistently taken a few supplements that I find support my health, including protein powder, probiotics and digestive enzymes, fish oil, vitamin D, B vitamins, and magnesium. I've also found it helpful to take a blend of supplements that support stress management, such as those containing ashwagandha or L-theanine.

This routine works well for me, but it's important to remember that each person's body is different and I have made modifications over the years. What works for one person might not work for another. The key is to listen to your body, adjust as needed, and be patient with the process. I have also worked personally with several natural health professionals such as nutritionist and naturopathic doctors over the years and still do today.

SLEEP: FUEL FOR MENTAL CLARITY & PHYSICAL HEALTH

It's no secret that sleep is essential, but many people don't realize just how critical it is for both physical recovery and mental clarity. During sleep, your body repairs muscles, restores energy, and strengthens your immune system. It's also a time when your brain processes and consolidates memories and clears out toxins that accumulate throughout the day.

When you don't get enough sleep, of course, your energy levels suffer, but so does your cognitive function, decision-making abilities, and mood.

In addition to the quantity of sleep, the routine you develop before bedtime is critical. I've found that what you feed your mind right before bed has a profound impact on your sleep quality and the thoughts and feelings you wake up with the next day. The thirty minutes before sleep is a powerful time for your subconscious mind, which is open and processing everything you've absorbed during the day. This is why I strongly recommend avoiding negative stimuli, such as the news or intense media, before bed.

Instead, I recommend dimming the lights, minimizing screen time, and engaging in light, uplifting activities. Read something inspiring or light-hearted, practice gratitude, or listen to a guided meditation. These simple practices allow your mind to wind down and prepare for a peaceful night's rest, which in turn supports mental clarity, immune function, and even muscle recovery.

Sleep is a time for your mind to rest and your body to heal, so make sure you're giving yourself the best conditions for both.

THE ROLE OF FOOD, FITNESS, & SLEEP IN LIVING FULLY

Your nutrition, movement, and rest play a vital role in how you show up in the world. They support your mood, energy, clarity, and ability to live fully.

When you feel good in your body, you're more equipped to give your best to your relationships, your work, and your purpose. You show up with more presence, more patience, and more possibility.

Food, fitness, and sleep are more than physical tools. They're acts of self-respect. When you consistently nourish your body and fuel your mind, you're affirming that you're worth the effort, worth the care it takes to live with energy, joy, and authenticity.

FINAL THOUGHTS:
THE LONG-TERM PATH TO HEALTH

In your journey toward health and well-being, it's important to approach nutrition and fitness as long-term, sustainable practices. There are no quick fixes, and it's definitely not about perfection. It's about making consistent, small changes over time that align with your values and goals.

Be open and unattached to rigid outcomes, doing your best with a spirit of kindness toward yourself as you learn and grow. Every step forward matters, and it's okay if the path takes time. Never give up on yourself, you are worth the effort, whatever it takes, and however long it takes.

Remember, health is not a destination, it's a journey. Be patient with yourself, stay curious, and continue evolving. Nourishing your body and fueling your mind is about more than what you eat and how you exercise. It's about embracing how you live, every single day.

And in the next chapter, we'll talk about another core pillar of living audaciously joyful, **your body language**. Because how you carry yourself in the world, your posture and presence send a message to others and also to your own subconscious about who you believe you are.

CHAPTER 11

HOW YOU SHOW UP

. . . .

BODY LANGUAGE & THE POWER OF PRESENCE

Body language speaks louder than words. It tells a story before you've said a single thing. The way you hold yourself, make eye contact, and engage physically with the world sends powerful signals to everyone around you. And here's the key: your body language is a direct reflection of your inner state, your confidence, your self-image, and the energy you carry into a space. By "energy," I'm referring to the felt sense people get when they're in your presence...your unspoken frequency. It can communicate authenticity, strength, and openness without a word being spoken.

In this chapter, we'll explore how mastering your body language can elevate the way you show up in every area of your life. This is where you begin to reflect joy, warmth, and presence, drawing people in simply by how you carry yourself. You'll discover how open body language not only builds stronger personal relationships, but also creates professional opportunities and deeper connections. When your inner state aligns with how you move through the world, your presence becomes a catalyst for influence, success, and joy.

BODY LANGUAGE & IDENTITY: THE ENERGY YOU PROJECT

Your body language begins with how you see yourself. It's a physical expression of your identity—the beliefs you hold about who you are, what you're capable of, and where you belong. When you feel grounded and authentic, your posture tends to reflect confidence and openness. When you doubt yourself, your body often mirrors that too through slouched shoulders, crossed arms, or a lack of eye contact.

Think about someone who walks into a room with their head held high, shoulders relaxed, and a calm, welcoming smile. Before they even speak, you can feel their confidence. That's the power of someone who is aligned with who they really are. When you embrace who you are and own your worth, your body language naturally becomes more magnetic and inviting.

And the good news is you can learn to carry yourself this way. The way you hold yourself can shift how you feel inside. By practicing strong, open postures like standing tall, making eye contact, and keeping your gestures relaxed, you're influencing how others see you. And you're also sending signals to your own nervous system that say, "I belong here." Over time, that outer shift helps reshape your inner reality.

As we touched on back in Chapter One, your energy enters the room before you do—and your body language is the physical expression of that energy.

"STANDING TALLER IN CORPORATE"

I remember a moment early in my corporate career when this truly clicked. I was about three years in and had started leading presentations to leaders in the company, sharing updates about product categories, performance results, and strategic plans. I looked young, I was small, and I was presenting to people who were often older, male, and much more experienced - some of them had been with the company for twenty years.

Even though I knew my material, I'd sometimes feel rattled when someone asked a question I didn't know how to answer. I'd shrink inside, suddenly feeling like I wasn't good enough to be at the front of the room. It's almost funny now, looking back, because today I'd handle that so differently. But back then, this was a turning point.

My boss at the time, Jason Blanchette, an incredible leader, noticed this and offered me something that made a huge impact. He reminded me: "Nicole, you are the expert in this room on this particular topic. Even if someone asks a question you don't know, you still likely know more than anyone here on this topic. Stand in that."

He encouraged me to stop overexplaining or softening my opinions with too much justification. "If you have a perspective," he said, "just say it. Say it with clarity and confidence. You don't need to add disclaimers."

Then he helped me visualize the room I was speaking to—standing tall, making eye contact, and owning the space; visualizing how the audience would be listening intently and interested in what I was sharing. I started changing how I carried myself. I looked around the room differently, stood taller, and spoke more clearly.

It was a full-body shift: part energy, part identity, part posture. And the results were profound. I noticed people listened more intently, engaged more thoughtfully, and respected my leadership in a new way. My body language wasn't only a reflection of my growing confidence; it became the tool that helped build it.

PRESENCE WITH AUTHENTICITY

That experience also taught me something deeper. There's nothing wrong with choosing to *look* confident even when you're feeling nervous inside. That's not inauthentic, it's courageous. The goal isn't to fake it, but to use intentional body language as a bridge between where you are and where you want to be. Over time, as you build belief and shift your internal dialogue, your outer posture and inner truth begin to align. That's when your confidence feels real, rooted, and unshakable.

Trying to be someone you're not creates disconnection, not just with others, but with yourself. That kind of presence may look polished on the outside, but it rarely lands with impact. On the other hand, when you show up as yourself, real, present, even imperfect, people feel it. That's what builds trust and true influence.

THE SOCIAL IMPACT OF CLOSED BODY LANGUAGE

These days, it's becoming increasingly common for people to disconnect physically, often unintentionally. The rise of technology and constant device use has created a culture of closed body language. Whether it's hunching over a smartphone, crossing arms while scrolling through social media, or avoiding eye contact in public, our body language is signaling disengagement, distraction, and sometimes, unapproachability. We see it everywhere - at coffee shops, in waiting rooms, even at social gatherings where people are physically present but mentally distant, glued to their screens.

The impact of this trend is profound. Closed body language makes it harder for others to start conversations or connect with you. It's easy to miss opportunities for meaningful interactions when your body is signaling that you're not available. Whether in social settings, at work, or even within your family, body language is key to connection. When people avoid eye contact, cross their arms, or look down at their phones, it creates a barrier to communication. These subtle signals say, "I'm not open to interacting."

And yet, deep connection is what we all crave. Our souls are wired for it. We need to connect with others to achieve our goals, to grow, and to find fulfillment. Whether it's in your personal life, professional network, or friendships, those meaningful relationships start with openness, and openness starts with your body language.

Even something as simple as lifting your head, putting down your phone, and making eye contact can dramatically shift the energy of an interaction. These small choices invite presence, signal availability, and quietly say, "I'm here, and I see you."

TURNING AWARENESS INTO CHANGE

By now, you might be thinking, *"Yes, I already know this."* You probably do. You know open body language makes you more approachable. You know constantly checking your phone sends a message of disconnection. And yet habits are powerful. Knowing isn't always enough to create change.

So how do you actually shift this?

Start with something small. The next time you're waiting in line or sitting in a meeting, resist the urge to automatically reach for your phone. Instead, look up. Breathe. Make eye contact with someone. Even *noticing* your posture in that moment and choosing to shift it is a win.

If you want more on how to change your default behaviors, go back and reread Chapter 5. That's where we talk about how small, intentional shifts, when repeated consistently, can rewire your habits and reshape your identity. This is one of those moments. Start with presence, and let that presence become your new normal.

OPEN BODY LANGUAGE: CREATING CONNECTION & OPPORTUNITY

Open body language can be simple to practice, and it can lead to immediate shifts in how people perceive and approach you. These small adjustments can help you radiate confidence, warmth, and openness. Here are a few practical ways to demonstrate open body language that encourages connection:

- **Uncross your arms and legs:** When you're sitting or standing, keep your limbs uncrossed. Crossed arms or legs send a subtle signal of defensiveness or discomfort. An open posture, on the other hand, invites people in and makes you more approachable.

- **Face people directly:** In conversation, angle your body toward the person you're speaking with. This nonverbal cue shows you're fully present and makes the other person feel seen and valued.

- **Make eye contact:** It's one of the simplest and most powerful ways to build connection. Eye contact signals attentiveness and presence. Even a brief moment of genuine eye contact can deepen trust and spark a sense of connection. And I know this can sometimes feel vulnerable - take courage and look them in the eye.

• **Smile genuinely:** A warm, sincere smile can shift the energy of an entire interaction. It communicates kindness, approachability, and emotional availability. Even in passing moments like greeting someone in line or thanking a barista, a smile can brighten someone's day.

• **Use your hands openly:** Avoid keeping your hands in your pockets or folding them across your body. When speaking, use your hands naturally to emphasize points or express openness. Open palms are a subconscious sign of honesty and trustworthiness.

These small shifts may seem simple, but they carry big impact. When your body language is open, you're more likely to spark conversations, invite support, and open unexpected doors. People feel safer around you, and that's often the beginning of connection, opportunity, and influence.

EXAMPLES OF HOW BODY LANGUAGE ATTRACTS OPPORTUNITY

Let's look at how open body language can create opportunities in different contexts:
• **Professional Settings**: Imagine you're at a networking event. You see two people standing at a small table, one with arms crossed, looking down at their phone, and the other with an

open posture, smiling, and making eye contact with the people passing by. Who would you feel more comfortable approaching? Most likely, it's the person who is open and engaged. The same goes for job interviews or team meetings. When you display confident, open body language, people trust you more and are more likely to offer support or opportunities.

- **Personal Relationships**: In personal relationships, body language is crucial for building trust and intimacy. Whether it's a romantic partner, a family member, or a friend, your body language shows how present and available you are. Sitting face-to-face with your phone put away, maintaining eye contact, and showing openness in your posture sends the message that the other person is important to you. It creates a sense of safety and connection, allowing for deeper conversations and bonds.

- **Everyday Interactions**: Even in everyday situations like standing in line at a coffee shop or on a plane, your body language can invite new connections. A simple smile or open stance can lead to a conversation with a stranger that could open unexpected doors. You never know what opportunities await when you project openness and kindness in your daily life.

CREATING BOUNDARIES WITH BODY LANGUAGE

While open body language is important for connection, there are also times when it's necessary to set boundaries. Not every situation or person requires full openness. It's essential to listen to your intuition and discern when it's appropriate to be open and when you need to create space for yourself.

For example, if someone is invading your personal space or you're in a situation where you feel unsafe, your body language can reflect the boundaries you need. Crossing your arms or stepping back may be necessary to signal that you need space or that a conversation is over. Being mindful of your body language in these moments allows you to protect your energy while still communicating clearly.

CREATING JOY THROUGH BODY LANGUAGE

At the heart of this entire book is the idea that joy isn't just something you feel, it's something you create and share. Your body language plays a powerful role in how that joy is expressed in the world. When you stand tall, make eye contact, and smile with genuine warmth, you send signals of positivity and presence without needing to say a word.

Think about the impact you could have just by walking into a room with an open posture, a steady gaze, and an ease about you. People notice. They may not always articulate it, but your presence shifts the energy. You become someone others feel safe around, someone they're drawn to without knowing exactly why.

This is the power of embodied joy. By aligning your inner state with your outer presence, you naturally become someone who uplifts a room. Whether you're speaking on stage, having a one-on-one conversation, or simply standing in line at the grocery store, your body language becomes a tool for connection, lightness, and leadership.

CHAPTER 12

THE COMPANY YOU KEEP

HOW PEOPLE AMPLIFY EVERYTHING

Think about the last time something amazing happened in your life. Maybe you received big news, accomplished a personal goal, or had a spontaneous moment of joy. Who did you want to tell first? Whose face came to mind? Chances are, there's someone, or a few people, you naturally think to reach out to when something meaningful happens. That instinct to share is part of who we are.

We're wired for connection. Whether we're celebrating, dreaming, or navigating life challenges, we're not meant to do it alone. Our joy expands when it's shared. Our lives feel more complete when we're witnessed by people who get us.

Now, when you think about goals you've achieved, the breakthroughs you've had, the moments you've felt proud or fulfilled. Did you accomplish any of them entirely alone? Or can you trace the path back to someone who gave you a chance, opened a door, offered a kind word, sparked an idea, helped with childcare, introduced you to the right contact, or simply believed in you?

Your dreams will come to life with and through other people.

You may not always know who they'll be, but if you stay open, they'll appear. Sometimes, it's the unexpected mentor at a networking event. Other times, it's your new friend who happens to know a publisher. It might even be someone who challenges you, wakes something up in you, and helps you grow in ways you didn't plan for.

And beyond reaching your goals, connection is what makes those moments matter. A new home means more when you get to welcome people into it. A pool is lovely for your family, and even more fulfilling when it becomes a space where your son's friends laugh and splash on a summer afternoon. A business win tastes sweeter when you get to call a friend who truly gets what it took to get there.

As Brené Brown says, *"Connection is why we're here. It is what gives purpose and meaning to our lives."* And as you'll see in the research from the Blue Zones, those rare regions around the world with the highest number of healthy centenarians, strong social bonds, and a sense of community are just as essential to longevity as vegetables and movement.

You were never meant to live a joy-filled, purpose-driven life in isolation. And you were never meant to achieve your dreams through your own singular struggle.

This chapter is a celebration and a reminder of the power of people.

WHEN BELIEF IN YOU CHANGES YOUR TRAJECTORY

Some people leave a mark on your life by seeing your potential before you fully do and reminding you of it until you start to believe it, too.

One of those people for me was my former corporate manager, Jason Blanchette who I mentioned in the last chapter. I was about three years into my corporate career after university, still learning and finding my footing, when I had the gift of working under a leader who made me feel truly seen and capable. Jason had this rare ability to give me more than my fair share of the credit when things went well and less of my share of the blame when they didn't.

I remember times when I did something great, and he would proudly say, "Nicole did an amazing job here," even though I'd leaned on him heavily for support. And when I made mistakes, as we all do, he never threw me under the bus, not publicly, and not privately either. I trusted him. My husband and I actually worked with him at one point together before we were even dating, and years later, we invited Jason to our wedding. That's how much of an impact he made.

He built me up with his words, his trust, and his belief. That belief helped me grow into the leader I am now, someone who tries to pass on that same gift. I aim to give others more than their share of the credit and less than their share of the blame. To let them know it's safe to grow, safe to stretch, and safe to sometimes get it wrong.

Another turning point came through someone I didn't yet know: Bill Banta.

Years after I had seen the movie *The Secret*, I heard Bob Proctor's voice on a podcast, not a mindset podcast, but a nutrition one I used to follow. The host had invited Bob on because he was shifting his message to mindset, and I immediately recognized Bob's voice from *The Secret*. That interview lit a fire inside me. At the end, Bob invited listeners to attend a three-day seminar. I signed up immediately, and that event changed my life.

It was one of those moments when everything in me said, *"This is what I've been waiting for."* The concepts I learned over those three days, several of which are reflected throughout this book, opened a new world for me. I couldn't believe no one had taught us this in school! My son was only a few months old at the time, and I watched virtually, holding him in my arms and wondering how I would ever unsee what I had now seen.

At the end of that seminar, Bob said, "If you want to work with us, reach out." I did. And that's how I met Bill Banta.

Bill is one of the best listeners I've ever met. Our first calls were so powerful that I knew: I didn't want to be a client, I wanted to be part of this work. I wanted to become a consultant, to help others learn what I had just discovered.

And then came the part where he told me the investment: double-digit thousands of dollars. At the time, I was already in debt. I owed my parents a significant amount from my struggling retail business. I had a new baby. I said, "There's no way. No, I can't."

And I'm so deeply grateful that Bill didn't accept that as my final answer. He didn't pressure me, but he didn't let me shrink either. He heard what was beneath my words. He asked me, "Is this what you really want?" And I knew it was.

He helped me realize something that has stayed with me ever since: *When you truly decide, ways and means will appear.* Together, we explored options, and I made the decision. I borrowed the money. I asked my parents—again— and I'll never forget what they told me later when I asked why they said yes. They said, *"Because we believed that you believed you could do it."* That still brings tears to my eyes.

I paid every penny back years ago. But the lesson stays with me: our expansion, our growth, and our breakthroughs almost always involve people. People who challenge us, support us, believe in us, and sometimes open doors we didn't even know existed.

THE FREQUENCY OF THE PEOPLE AROUND YOU

One of the most powerful, and often overlooked, factors in personal transformation is the energy of the people you surround yourself with.

You've likely experienced this firsthand. When you're in the presence of high-frequency people, those who are grounded in possibility, growth, and integrity, you feel different. You're more inspired. You think bigger. You hold your shoulders a little higher. You take bolder action.

They don't do everything for you. You grow in who you *become* in their presence.

I've seen this happen in coaching rooms, both virtual and in person. I've felt it in mastermind conversations where one sentence from someone else can spark a breakthrough I'd been circling for months. And I've watched it happen to others, too. Sometimes it's a comment, an insight, or even just someone boldly sharing their dream that unlocks something for another person in the room. It might be a new idea, a fresh connection, or simply the realization that, *if they can go after that, maybe I can too.* I've felt it in casual conversations with friends who I would consider on a high frequency hold me to a higher standard by naturally inviting me to rise just by how they live and lead themselves.

The right people help you regulate your nervous system, clarify your vision, and take action with more certainty. They remind you what you're capable of. They normalize excellence, gratitude, and joy. They make growth feel less like a lonely path and more like a shared experience. One conversation can shift your entire trajectory. That's why the energy you surround yourself with is a powerful lever.

Who you're around is shaping what you do and also shaping what you believe is possible.

As Jim Rohn famously said, "You are the average of the five people you spend the most time with." Whether you fully agree with that or not, it's worth pausing to notice: Who's in your inner circle? Who do you turn to when you're dreaming big or doubting yourself? The people closest to you are influencing your standards, your language, your confidence, your expectations, and your vision. Sometimes, because they tell you what to do or what they think, and also because energy is contagious.

And when you consciously choose to surround yourself with people who live with purpose, gratitude, and alignment, something shifts. You grow faster and you grow with more joy.

WHAT HIGH-FREQUENCY REALLY MEANS

When I talk about high-frequency people, I don't mean those who are always bubbly or relentlessly positive. High frequency isn't about being upbeat 24/7 or forcing a smile when things are hard.

A high-frequency person is someone who is anchored. They often move through the world with calm, confidence, and compassion. They're present. They're grounded. They experience joy, peace, or excitement, and they're not reactive. They respond with intention. They can hold space for challenges without collapsing into complaint. They don't drain a room or dominate it, they elevate it.

They typically live in a state of abundance and possibility, whether consciously or instinctively. They're not overly competitive because they know there's enough to go around. They're not constantly striving to prove something, because they already know who they are.

This kind of energy is magnetic, safe, and expansive. And just as importantly, this frequency isn't fixed. It's not a personality type. It's a state you can return to, over and over, with practice, presence, and intention.

WHEN YOU'RE SURROUNDED BY NEGATIVITY

As you raise your own frequency, you may start to notice things you hadn't before, like how certain environments, conversations, or relationships feel heavy or draining. You might realize that some of the people around you tend to dwell on problems, complain constantly, criticize others, or see life through a lens of fear or lack. And at first, this realization can feel discouraging. You might think, "Wait, how did I not notice this before?"

That's okay. Awareness is a sign of growth.

There may be people in your life, coworkers, friends, or even family members, who are not in the same season of growth as you. You don't have to label them as wrong or bad. And you don't need to make abrupt decisions. But you *do* have a choice.

You can choose how much time and energy you invest in certain dynamics. You can choose what topics are off limits, how long you stay in a conversation, or when it's time to step away altogether. And sometimes, as your frequency rises, people will naturally fall away. You don't have to push them out; your energy simply no longer matches the environment you once shared.

You can also choose to hold your own frequency higher, even when you're surrounded by others who aren't doing the same. This is where many of the practices in this book, like gratitude, identity awareness, breath, and presence, become tools to shift you. They help you stay anchored in who you are, regardless of what's happening around you.

You don't have to become someone else to stay connected. And you don't have to sacrifice your growth in order to keep everyone comfortable. You have a choice. And every time you choose alignment, you create more of it for yourself and for others who are watching, wondering, and maybe ready to rise, too.

THE POWER OF VULNERABILITY

There's a moment when you decide to let someone see you, not just the polished parts, but the parts that are still in progress. And that's the moment true connection begins.

Some of the most meaningful relationships in my life were deepened through vulnerability. And some of the most powerful opportunities I've had came after I shared something real, not something impressive.

People trust you more when they see your humanity. They're drawn to your authenticity. Vulnerability doesn't make you weaker. It makes you more relatable, more magnetic, and more trustworthy. If you're willing to go first, to be honest about what you're navigating, it gives others permission to show up more fully, too. That's where connection deepens and impact begins.

It's easy to think we need to show the highlight reel in order to earn people's respect. But over and over, I've seen the opposite. Some of the moments where people felt most connected to me, whether clients, audiences, or even close friends, weren't after I shared a win. They were after I shared a failure.

There's something powerful about saying, "Here's where I messed up. Here's what I learned. And here's how I'm growing from it."

It reminds people that they're not alone. That growth is messy. That success isn't linear. And that you don't have to be perfect to be inspiring, you have to be real.

START WITH YOU: BECOMING THE PERSON YOU WANT TO FIND

If you've ever felt like you don't have the right people around you, whether in friendship, love, leadership, or collaboration, one of the most powerful places to begin is with yourself.

Start with you. Start by becoming the type of person you want to find.

If you're looking for a team member who is dependable, engaged, driven, and values growth, embody those traits in how you show up. If you're hoping to meet a romantic partner who is confident, kind, and aligned, practice being that energy now. If you're calling in new friendships that are uplifting and real, be that friend to others, and to yourself.

Energy multiplies. The people who are meant for you will recognize your frequency. You won't have to chase them because you're living it.

You might be surprised by how quickly connection finds its way back to you. Even small moments matter. A genuine smile. A thoughtful comment on someone's post. Holding the door and making eye contact. These may seem insignificant, but they carry frequency, and that frequency draws a connection in return.

This idea first took root in me years ago when I read something from Neale Donald Walsch in *Conversations with God*. He wrote that when you want something for yourself, offer it to another. That simple concept has reshaped how I show up in the world. When I want more encouragement, I give it. When I'm seeking support, I offer it. When I feel a bit low, I help someone else rise. And again and again, I've seen how that energy finds its way back unexpectedly and beautifully.

And when you live this way intentionally, something begins to shift at the core. You remember who you are.

The founder of Elevated Worldwide, Tony Child teaches that there is a difference between thinking abundance and *living* abundance and how remembering who you really are influences who you bring into your life. Here's how he describes it:

Living abundance is seen in all areas of life, and it shows up as a vibrant, powerful, and real energy.
It shows up in love, as forgiveness.
It shows up in time, as being present.

It shows up in money, as generosity.
It shows up in health, as complete wellness.
It shows up in careers, as engagement.
It shows up in spirituality, as power.
It shows up in you, as always enough.

You are more than enough.
You are beautiful, courageous, and bold.
You are faithful, loving, and forgiving.
It is in your nature to be this way.
Cynicism, skepticism, and pessimism are learned
and inherited from previous generations.
People are not born with these traits, they're learned.
You were born with optimism, courage, and strong belief.

Let that land for a moment.

You were born with optimism. You were born with courage. You were born with strong belief.

The work of this book has been about remembering that truth. And the invitation that follows is simple: start living from it.

In the next section, the epilogue, you'll read one final story that ties it all together. It's a story of bold action, radical trust, and living from your joy, even when the path looks uncertain. I hope you'll keep reading.

Because you're right on the edge of living audaciously joyful.

SAY YES TO LIFE

There comes a moment, sometimes quiet, sometimes electric, when you feel the invitation.

To leap. To decide. To say yes before you're "ready."

That's what this book has been building toward: Inner clarity, healing, and joy, but also the courage to act from it.

Living audaciously joyful is not passive. It's even more than feeling light and peaceful on the inside. Living audaciously is about making moves that align with who you really are, even when they scare you. Especially when they scare you.

Sometimes, that looks like leaving a corporate job without knowing exactly what's next. Sometimes, it's investing in yourself when the numbers don't fully make sense yet. Sometimes, it's saying yes to a TEDx talk, a new business, a new relationship, or a chance that feels wild and exhilarating.

Other times, it's simply choosing to speak up, be seen, or follow a creative urge.

This is boldness. And joy grows through it.

I'll never forget the firewalk.

It was at the fourth weekend of a personal development event I attended a couple of years ago. I had heard about walking barefoot across hot coals before, but I always assumed it was for people who were a little out there, or had something to prove. Still, I was curious. I showed up open but a bit fearful.

That night, we were led through breathwork, visualization, and mindset exercises. As the fire was lit and the sky darkened, something began to shift. It wasn't about proving anything. It was about remembering.

I didn't walk on fire because I'm fearless. I walked because I was ready to meet a part of myself I had forgotten.

And I did.

That moment, walking barefoot across hot coals without hesitation or injury, shattered something I didn't even realize was holding me back. It wasn't just physical. It was emotional, spiritual, and identity-shaking. The truth hit me:

You only believe something is impossible until you realize it's not.

Afterward, our firewalk instructor invited us to write a declaration. Mine has stayed taped to the mirror in my bathroom ever since:

**"The impossible is possible. I walked on fire.
I can accomplish anything I choose."**

I read it every day. Not to hype myself up. To *remember*. To remember that I am already powerful, whole, and free.

This entire book has been about that remembering. Remembering who you are at your core, creative, joyful, capable, connected, and complete. Reconnecting with that childlike lightness, trusting your intuition, and learning to let go of the stories that kept you small.

Now, it's time to live from that place.

You don't need to see the full staircase to take the first step. You don't need all the money, all the plans, all the proof. You need to decide. And then trust that the dots will connect.

Bob Proctor used to say that you don't need the money to do something, you need the decision. The money shows up *after* the committed decision is made. It's a bold idea, but it's one I've lived. And every time I've honored it, new possibilities opened up.

I'm not saying every leap will feel safe. Boldness almost always wakes up old stories, fear, and doubt. It stretches your identity. It challenges your paradigms. But that's where your next level lives, in motion.

Tony Child calls it, "Fire. Then aim. Then ready." It flips the order most of us are taught. It's bold. And it's how breakthroughs happen and it's how you live audaciously joyful.

You won't always feel fully ready. You won't have every answer. Bold action is about trust. It's about showing up for your life, right now, as the fullest version of who you are.

You've already done so much work.

Now the next part is simple.

Live it.

Say yes.

NICOLE KERNOHAN

Nicole Kernohan is a TEDx Speaker, bestselling author, and high-performance coach who has spent more than a decade helping entrepreneurs and business leaders unlock their potential. She is a partner with Elevated Worldwide, an international coaching company that blends positive psychology and proven success principles to create breakthroughs in business and life.

Nicole earned her coaching certification through the Elevated Coaching Academy (International Coaching Federation accredited) and was a certified consultant with Bob Proctor's Proctor Gallagher Institute Thinking Into Results program. She studied positive psychology through Yale University's Science of Well-Being course and earned an

Honors Business degree from Wilfrid Laurier University in Ontario, Canada. She also earned a Nutritional Practitioner designation, integrating her passion for health and vitality with her work in personal and professional transformation.

Her insights and coaching work have been featured in Success magazine, Forbes, and iHeartRadio. She is also a co-author of the bestselling *Book of Human Empowerment* series.

At age twenty, Nicole was diagnosed with multiple sclerosis and temporarily paralyzed. Instead of collapsing under fear and limitation, she devoted herself to the study of the mind, body, and spirit. She has now lived healthfully for more than twenty years, modelling the resilience and joy she teaches.

Whether on stage, in coaching rooms, or through her writing, she empowers people to live with freedom, authenticity, and audacious joy.

www.NicoleKernohan.com

Sources & Suggested Reading

The ideas in *Audacious Joy* have been shaped by my own journey as well as the wisdom of extraordinary teachers, mentors, leaders, and writers who have influenced the world of personal and professional development. The works listed here span timeless success principles, powerful lessons in identity and mindset, spiritual and visionary insights, and modern approaches to resilience and growth. You'll notice that many of them could fit into more than one category because truth rarely stays in one tidy box (and honestly, neither should we). My encouragement is to follow what speaks to you most. Let curiosity be your compass, and see where these voices guide you.

Timeless Foundations of Success

- **Napoleon Hill.** *Think and Grow Rich.* First published 1937.

- **Sharon Lechter & Greg Reid.** *Three Feet from Gold: Turn Your Obstacles into Opportunities.* Sterling Publishing, 2009.

- **Sharon Lechter.** *Think and Grow Rich for Women: Using Your Power to Create Success and Significance.* TarcherPerigee, 2014.

- **Wallace D. Wattles.** *The Science of Getting Rich.* First published 1910.

- **Florence Scovel Shinn.** *The Game of Life and How to Play It.* First published 1925.

- **David J. Schwartz.** *The Magic of Thinking Big.* Simon & Schuster, 1959.

Mindset, Identity & Growth

- **Dr. Maxwell Maltz.** *Psycho-Cybernetics*. Prentice-Hall, 1960.

- **Bob Proctor.** *You Were Born Rich*. Proctor Gallagher Institute, 1984.

- **Price Pritchett.** *You²: A High Velocity Formula for Multiplying Your Personal Effectiveness in Quantum Leaps*. Pritchett Publishing, 1994.

- **John C. Maxwell.** *The 15 Invaluable Laws of Growth: Live Them and Reach Your Potential*. Center Street, 2012.

- **Marcus Buckingham & Donald O. Clifton.** *Now, Discover Your Strengths*. Free Press, 2001.

- **Les Brown.** *Live Your Dreams*. William Morrow, 1992.

Vision, Spirit & Inner Wisdom

- **Dr. Joe Vitale.** *The Attractor Factor: 5 Easy Steps for Creating Wealth (or Anything Else) From the Inside Out*. Wiley, 2005.

- **Neale Donald Walsch.** *Conversations with God* (series). Putnam Books, beginning 1995.

- **Oprah Winfrey.** *What I Know for Sure*. Flatiron Books, 2014.

Modern Perspectives on Habits & Resilience

- **Brené Brown.** *The Gifts of Imperfection*. Hazelden, 2010.

- **James Clear.** *Atomic Habits: An Easy & Proven Way to Build Good Habits & Break Bad Ones*. Avery, 2018.

- **Mel Robbins.** *The 5 Second Rule*. Savio Republic, 2017.

Mentors & Partners Who Inspire Me

- **Tony Child.** Teachings from GratiShift™ and Elevated Worldwide programs.

- **Bill Banta.** Leadership insights and coaching through Elevated Alliance.

www.ingramcontent.com/pod-product-compliance
Lightning Source LLC
Chambersburg PA
CBHW042315120626

46547CB00022B/2111